CANALS
of Shropshire

Richard K Morriss

Shropshire
Books

Front Cover: A wooden lift bridge at Whixall on the Prees branch of the
                Ellesmere Canal. (Photograph by Alex Ingram)
Back Cover: The Ellesmere Canal near Colemere
                (Photograph by Gordon Dickins)

ISBN 0 - 903802 - 47 - 3 © Text Richard K Morriss 1991. Reprinted 1998
Cover and book design by Paul Brasenell
Illustration by Richard Whitfield
Editing by Helen Sample
Published by Shropshire Books, the publishing imprint of Shropshire County Council's
Community and Economic Services Division.
Printed in Great Britain by Precision Colour Printing Ltd. Telford.

This book is dedicated to the memory of my late grandparents,
Richard and Violet Martin

Contents

Acknowledgements

Work has progressed on this book, on and off, for several years and in that time I have been helped and encouraged by many people. I would like to thank, yet again, Anthony Carr and Richard Preston and the other staff of the Local Studies Library, Shrewsbury, for their enthusiasm; the staff of the County Record Offices of Shropshire and of Hereford & Worcester; the Public Record Office, Kew; the Boat Museum, Ellesmere Port; the Waterways Museum, Stoke Bruerne; the British Waterways Board; Ken Hoverd for last minute photographic help; the Ironbridge Gorge Museum Trust; and the staff and former colleagues of the Ironbridge Institute. The moral support and good natured patience of friends and relations is unquantifiable but essential. I am indeed indebted to so many, but in particular to my parents, my brother and his family, Joan and her clan, and last, but certainly not least, to Ruth.

Richard K Morriss

The publisher would like to thank the following organisations and individuals for permission to reproduce the illustrations in this book:

British Waterways Archives (Glos.) pp 24,28; Shrewsbury, Local Studies Library pp xii, 6, 9, 12, 16, 17, 19, 26, 31, 34, 36, 53, 56, 60, 66, 68, 69; R.E James p 2; Ironbridge Gorge Museum Trust pp 4,5,7,22; The Shropshire Magazine p 29; J.E.J. Whitaker p 32; Ordnance Survey p 37; Richard K. Morriss pp 20,22,39,42,44,46,59,62,64,71,72,74, 76,81; Francis Frith Collection, Birmingham Library p 51; A.P. Wallace p 54; H. Harris p 33; C. G. Harper "The Holyhead Road" p 48; W. Preen p 28 (top); S.R. Turner p 78 (bottom); Harold Griffiths, p 40; S. M. Sonsino p 14.
The photographs were reproduced by Steve Ryal.

About the Author

Richard Morriss grew up in North Staffordshire and first became interested in canals playing by the remains of the long-abandoned Uttoxeter Branch near his home in Alton. One of his earliest memories of Shropshire is of paddling a canvas canoe in the pouring rain from Wolverhampton to Market Drayton and back along the 'Shroppie' in the late 1960's. Ten years later, after various jobs, including driving a miniature train on Margate pier and salmon netting in Scotland, he returned to the county to visit a friend - and has stayed ever since.

A lifelong interest in architecture has become a career and after working for English Heritage and the Ironbridge Gorge Museum, he is now Assistant Director of the Hereford Archaeology Unit, specialising in surveying historic buildings throughout the Welsh Marches. Along the way he has obtained Masters degrees in English Literature and in Industrial Archaeology and his books include 'Railways of Shropshire' (Shropshire Libraries 1983) and 'Rail Centres: Shrewsbury', (Ian Allan 1986). A book on the Shropshire and Montgomeryshire Railway is nearing completion and he has also written numerous articles on architecture, archaeology and transport.

Other interests include walking, travel and photography. He still canoes, occasionally, and has swum down some of the best rapids in Britain. When pressed, he will also admit to being a supporter of Shrewsbury Town Football Club.

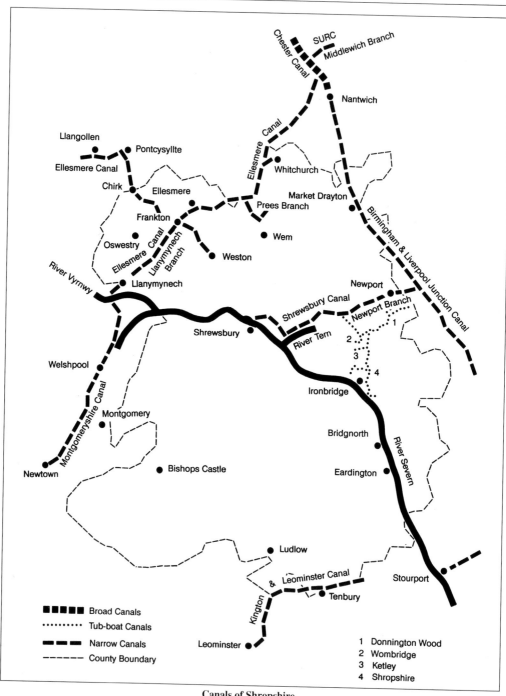

Canals of Shropshire

Foreword

One of the people responsible for popularising the delights of the Ironbridge area was the great canal and transport writer, L.T.C. Rolt. His visits here during the war were followed by successful attempts by Allied Ironfounders in the 1950's to preserve some of the industrial history of the area. Ironbridge is now one of the leading industrial Museums in the World, and it is therefore surprising that no-one has written a book specifically on the canals of Shropshire. Richard K Morriss, who attended the Ironbridge Institute during 1986/87 has now redressed this problem. The Institute offers post-graduate degrees in industrial archaeology and heritage management. It is therefore highly appropriate that Richard should produce this excellent book on this aspect of our industrial history.

The development of industrial Shropshire, and the Ironbridge Gorge in particular, was dependent on the navigation of the River Severn and then on the growth of canal systems which brought goods from the hinterland down to the river. In the eighteenth century, travel was difficult for everyone and, without river and canal navigation, was nigh impossible. This book traces the development of canals throughout the area starting off with a fascinating chapter on river navigation.

The Ironbridge Gorge Museum attempts to portray some of this history through its displays, particularly at the Museum of the River which shows a model of the River Severn between Dale End and Coalport as it was on the 12th August 1796. At Blists Hill the last Severn Trow, the Spry, is now nearing the final stages of restoration and will soon be moored on the river to indicate the scale of river traffic.

The last vestiges of the east Shropshire canal system are preserved through Blists Hill with the Inclined Plane at Coalport. Plans also exist to extend the canal from Coalport Canal Basin through to Coalport Bridge. A further canal structure in the County of unique interest is the aqueduct at Longden-on-Tern now preserved by English Heritage as an ancient monument. Whilst a few navigable canals still exist in the County, it is to be hoped that this book will be one factor which might rekindle interest in our canals and their history, and I warmly recommend you to read on.

Stuart B. Smith, Director Ironbridge Gorge Museum.

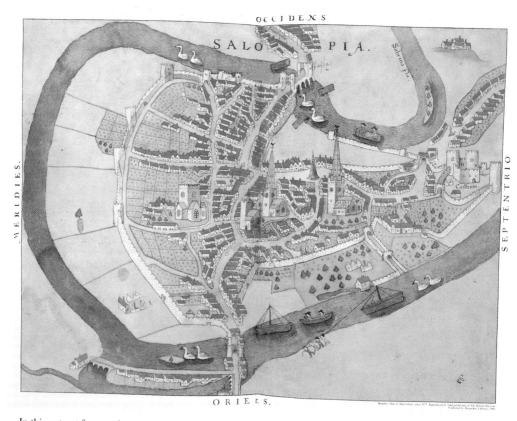

In this extract from a nineteeth century copy of the late sixteeth century map of Shrewsbury, bowhauliers tow a barge up towards the English Bridge, in Shrewsbury, apparently unworried by the giant swans behind them.

Rivers

On a summer day, watching children paddling in the shallows of the Severn by Bridgnorth bridge, it is difficult to believe that this town was once one of the important river ports of England and that dozens of barges loaded and unloaded their cargoes at its busy quays. It is perhaps even more difficult to realise that some of those barges travelled on up the river almost as far as Welshpool.

Nevertheless, until the latter part of the eighteenth century the rivers were the main inland highways of the kingdom, and the only means by which any large cargoes could be carried safely, quickly and economically over long distances. Roads, poorly maintained since the departure of the Romans, were little better than rough and rutted tracks in dry summers and impassable quagmires in wet winters. The long established tradition of inland navigation on rivers would eventually lead to the creation of the national canal network.

The Severn was the longest navigable river in the country. Because of the rich farmland through which it flowed and the industries that grew up near to its banks, it also became the most important. Little is known about the use of the Severn or other local rivers in prehistoric times, although a dug-out canoe recently found on the banks of the Meese near to Newport has been carbon dated to around 1300 BC and dug-outs found in the meres around Ellesmere may also date to the Bronze Age.

The Romans almost certainly made use of the Severn, as did the Saxons, but the first documented use of the river occurs in the twelfth century when lead was shipped downstream from the mines around Shelve to Gloucestershire. The first recorded passenger was the wife of Griffin ap Rese, and the cost of hiring the barge that took her from Bridgnorth to Gloucester in 1198 was 6s 3d (31½p), then quite a considerable sum.

By the thirteenth and fourteenth centuries the river trade was flourishing. Local produce taken by river included timber from West Shropshire and the borderlands, floated downstream in rafts or 'flottes'. Most of this was for the building trade or for domestic firewood, but some would have been used as fuel in fledgling brewing and iron making industries developing near to the river. the monks of Buildwas exported wool from their flocks by barge to Bristol, from where some of it was sent as far afield as Italy. Amongst the cargoes travelling upstream from the estuary were Spanish leather, wine, wrought iron and tin. In 1270 cargoes of stone were carried by river to pave the streets of Shrewsbury.

Despite, or perhaps because of, the growing river trade there were continuous battles between the barge owners and the owners of the land through which the river flowed. Statutes of Henry VI and Henry VIII had stipulated that the river - the 'King's high stream of Severn' - and its towpaths should be free of all tolls, and in 1449 a water bailiff was appointed to keep the navigation open and regulate its use. Despite this legal protection, landowners could still obstruct the river by building weirs across it.

Although the Severn, with its unpredictable fluctuation of water levels, was not a very suitable river for corn, leather or fulling mills, it was a very productive source of a staple medieval foodstuff - fish. In order to catch large amounts of fish, landowners built fish weirs across the river at suitable points. Four such weirs are mentioned in the Domesday Survey of 1086. The fish weirs were put across where the river bed was gravelly and shallow and were usually built in a 'V' shape, pointing downstream, though the larger weirs had more than one 'V'. They were made of a timber framework of piles and beams into which slotted a series of wattle panels. The fish were funnelled into the 'V' and caught in a net; a catwalk over the whole weir gave access to the nets. It was a simple and efficient method of catching salmon and eel in particular.

Obviously it caused disruption to the river traffic. Special bypass channels, known as barge gutters, were built around the weir on the main towpath side of the river. These gutters, often several hundred yards long, were, in many ways, miniature canals and resulted in a series of long islands between themselves and the true course of the river, called 'bylets'. There were still problems, particularly in dry summers, and many

The fish weir at Preston Boats near Uffington was the last in the county, surviving until the 1920's, and was said to date back to Saxon times.

complaints from barge owners. A special Commission in 1575 found that there were no less than forty fish weirs on the Shropshire Severn but most were out of use by the end of the following century. By the mid-nineteenth century there were only four left and the last of these, at Preston Boats near Shrewsbury, was badly damaged in the floods of 1910 and dismantled in the 1920's.

The river traffic had continued to expand throughout the sixteenth century, mostly for goods traffic but occasionally for passengers. For example in 1581 the Lord President of the Marches of Wales, Sir Henry Sidney, 'took hys Barge under the Cassell Hyll' in Shrewsbury and travelled part of the way to Ludlow on the river, stopping to entertain local dignitaries on board at Atcham.

Increasing traffic meant the expansion of old wharves and the building of new ones. In Bridgnorth the Old Quay by the bridge had been in use since medieval times but Foster's Loade was probably built in the 1580's. In Shrewsbury Rowland Jenks opened Mardol Quay, by the Welsh Bridge, in 1607. Like most of the others it was a public wharf and he was to 'permit all manner of barges of all persons, to load at the said quay, taking for every barge load of wood or coal, twelve pence; for a ton of other goods off a Burgess, two pence; and off a foreigner, four pence'. It was followed by a quay on the opposite bank, in Frankwell, in 1608.

Before the monks at Strata Marcella had built a stone weir near Welshpool in late medieval times, the river may still have been navigable further upstream when the water level was high enough. By the start of the seventeenth century a New Quay had been built below the weir which later became known as Pool Quay, and dealt mainly with the Montgomeryshire timber trade, which continued well into the nineteenth century. The timber was widely used in shipbuilding, particularly by the Royal Navy.

The volume of traffic increased even more rapidly during the eighteenth century. The Severn was a key element in the phenomenal industrial growth of East Shropshire. Once Abraham Darby had perfected the use of coal in the iron smelting process early in the century, the combination of coal and iron deposits, water power from the streams running into the river, and the transport facilities offered by the Severn, helped to change the world.

The rapid expansion of coal mining in the area led to a considerable increase in the amount of coal carried on the river, for both domestic and industrial use. About a hundred thousand tons was carried each year up or downstream from the Gorge area by the middle of the eighteenth century, when the river was one of the busiest in Europe. Iron goods from the Gorge area were also sent away by river, and pig iron, mostly from the Forest of Dean area, was brought in to be used by the local iron industry. The other main cargoes downstream at this time still included wool, as well as grain, hops and cider. Amongst the goods coming upstream were luxuries such as sugar, tea, coffee and wine.

Loadcroft or Ludcroft Wharf, Coalbrookdale, was the terminus of the Coalbrookdale Company's plateway system and this photograph of circa 1860 shows how plateway wagons ran onto the wharf ready to be loaded into waiting barges or trows.

The riverbanks in the Gorge were lined with wharves, linked to the various mines, quarries and factories by fairly primitive, but efficient, wooden waggonways - the forerunners of the modern railway. The river was often crowded with craft of all kinds, loading or unloading, or waiting to get to the wharves. Jackfield, towards the southern end of the Gorge, was where most of the watermen and owners in the area lived.

The vessels using the river always varied considerably in size, but by the eighteenth century the main cargo carriers were roughly divided into trows or barges; the distinction between the two was more to do with size than design. The trows were large flat-bottomed craft with rounded bilges which evolved over the years to reach their heyday towards the end of the eighteenth century. Trows are mentioned as early as 1411 when several trow owners were accused of forming a confederacy to raise prices to such an extent that some traders risked using makeshift rafts to carry their wares, which were in turn set upon by thugs hired by the trow owners.

By the eighteenth century, trows, often up to sixty foot long and weighing over eighty tons, could, work between the Ironbridge Gorge and the Bristol Channel, the larger ones capable of hugging the coast as far as Bristol itself. They seldom worked up to Shrewsbury; most traffic from that town was carried in barges, or frigates, usually single masted vessels between forty and sixty foot long. These rarely ventured further downstream than Gloucester, which became an important transhipment point for any cargoes going further down river. Usually the vessel would be manned by its owner and two or three watermen. Some barge owners would have two or three vessels but larger fleets were uncommon. Even companies such as the Coalbrookdale Company mainly used independent owners rather than owning many vessels themselves.

Thomas Beard's 'William' was one of the last trows on the Shropshire Severn and is seen here at Jackfield in the 1880's.

The trows and barges were built for goods traffic. Passengers were taken in much smaller, lighter and faster craft called wherries, seldom displacing more than a few tons. They could be rowed by up to eight oarsmen and there were regular wherry services plying the Severn in the early eighteenth century. In March 1750 Captain William Owen described in his journal how, en route from Llanidloes to London, he left Shrewsbury 'on board the Wherry, breakfasted at Atcham, dined at Bridgnorth, drank tea at Bewdley and at nine o'clock at night arrived at Worcester'.

The smallest craft of all was, and occasionally still is, the coracle, described in 1645 as 'a little boate for one to sitte in; they call them corricles, laths within and leather without, from corium'.
The coracle is probably one of the most ancient designs of craft still afloat and has certainly been in use since Saxon times, either for fishing or simply for crossing from one bank to the other. They were not designed for long distance travelling, although an eighty year old Shropshire man named Peplow was said to have paddled his coracle from Shrewsbury to Worcester in the 1790's to catch a glimpse of King George the Third, who was visiting the city.

Tommy Rogers carrying one of his coracles at Ironbridge in the early nineteen hundreds.

Most of the craft using the river were built along its banks and there were flourishing barge building yards in Shrewsbury, the Ironbridge Gorge, Bridgnorth and Quatford. Many of these craft were very long lived. The fully rigged trow 'William' (one of many of that name) was built at the Bower Yard, Broseley, in 1809 and was the oldest British trading vessel in service in June 1939, when she finally foundered in the Severn estuary. The 'Severn', built in Bridgnorth in 1752, was said to have been in service in Carrickfergus as late as 1883 making her even longer lasting.

One of the world's first iron boats was built by the ironmaster John 'Iron-Mad' Wilkinson at the Willey Ironworks and launched nearby in 1787. The 'Trial' was essentially an eight ton narrowboat similar to those on the new canals, and was made of wrought iron plates. Much to people's surprise she floated, and her maiden voyage was down the river and along canals to Birmingham. Later in the year an iron barge was built for the Severn traffic but was not a great success, and most craft on the river continued to be built of timber.

The Bower Yard in the Ironbridge Gorge was one of the last boat building yards on the upper river to close.

Not all of the craft built in Shropshire were destined for the upper Severn traffic, particularly in the nineteenth century. Another Bridgnorth built 'Severn', a 166 ton brig launched in 1850 when the river traffic was in rapid decline, traded to the Baltic; and another Bridgnorth brig, the 135 ton 'Gleanor' of 1855 sailed to South America and the West Indies. The last boat built in the town was launched in 1868.

Shrewsbury's barge building industry had declined by the start of the nineteenth century but the last to be built there was launched as late as 1858. Ironically, this was a 44 ft. steam barge built at Coleham by the Severn Valley Railway to help in the construction of a line that finally killed off the last vestiges of the river trade. On a lighter note, a Shrewsbury boat builder, R. Ellis, received an unusual order to build nine boats for the pantomime 'Babes in the Wood' being staged at the Queen's Theatre, Manchester. The order came on the 23rd December 1886, and they were ready for the Boxing Day premiere.

Although equipped with masts and capable of using sails in favourable conditions, trows and barges seldom used them. Going downstream was usually simple enough, with the craft being carried by the current and steered. Going upstream was a different, and more expensive, matter. In the mid-eighteenth century the cargo rate between Shrewsbury and Bristol, for example, was 10/- (50p) per ton; the rate upstream was 15/- (75p).

The riverside paths were specifically mentioned in the early river legislation because they were used as towpaths. Despite the extent of the river trade on the upper Severn these paths continued to be badly maintained until the end of the eighteenth century and were unfit for horses. Instead it was left to gangs of men, bowhauliers, to tow the trows and barges upstream. It was hard and often degrading work for these men, who seemed to have acquired a reputation for drunkenness, thieving and poaching amongst the people who lived along the river, and the bargeowners. The ironmaster Richard Reynolds described bowhauling in the 1770's as 'degrading and unseemly' but was equally concerned that it was 'the means of harbouring and collecting persons of bad character and facilitating a system of plunder injurious to the trade and destructive of the morals of the people engaged in it'.

In the mid-eighteenth century there were plans to make a proper horse towpath along the Severn, but a company set up by Act in 1772 failed to get anything done. William Reynolds built his own horse towpath from the Meadow Wharf in Coalbrookdale to the new settlement of Coalport in 1796. Then, in 1799, a new Act was passed that revived the old one and the path was ready by August 1800. Tolls were high, costing 6d per horse per mile, but its success led to another Act, in 1809, enabling the towpath to be extended upstream to Shrewsbury. This was opened by December and finished at Frankwell Quay, and probably led to the rebuilding of the New Union Wharf near to the castle in 1823.

Ironically the end of the river traffic was already in sight. Virtually unaltered by man, apart from the vastly reduced numbers of fish weirs and some dredging work, the upper Severn was very much a natural transport artery and, as such, subject to natural forces. In times of drought, the low water levels often meant that barges could be stranded for weeks at a time. High water meant hazardous journeys, and the river was, and still tragically is, potentially dangerous at any level.

An empty barge waits by the old Welsh Bridge, Shrewsbury, in 1778.
The large rudder was an asset for craft in slow waters.

Accidents, even in these placid waters, were frequent and often fatal: in 1761 two people on the Bridgnorth Wherry were drowned at Bewdley; on the same day in 1768 a barge was lost at Quatford and another 'sunk and dashed to pieces' at Madeley; and a flotte loaded with coal capsized near Edgerley in 1804 and one of its crew drowned. Most mishaps were caused by foolhardiness. For example in 1599, three members of the same family attempted to 'shoot' the old Welsh Bridge in Shrewsbury but their barge broadsided against the piers, capsized, and two were drowned. In 1776 a man saw his hat fall into the river whilst he was on a barge passing through Sutton Maddock; he leapt in after it - and drowned. At Alveley in 1789 a drunk on one of the horse ferries fell in and met that same unfortunate fate.

Although the Severn was by far the most important navigable river in the county, the lower reaches of several of its tributaries were also used from time to time. The River Vyrnwy could be used in good water levels as far upstream as Clawdd Coch to take away the local lead ore, and in the eighteenth century, iron from Bersham was carried here by pack horse. Considerable amounts of local limestone were shipped from Llanymynech, with 8,000 tons being taken away by barge in 1795 for example, as well as lead and zinc ores.

The River Tern flows through Attingham Park before joining the Severn but for the first half of the eighteenth century there was a busy forge here, called Tern Forge, and several more upstream. Tern Forge was one of the largest in the country and was served by small boats. A lock was built near to the confluence of the Severn, remains of which still survive, but it was very small and could only have allowed boats 23 ft. long and 7 ft. 8 ins. wide. The iron needed for the forge came from the Ironbridge Gorge or from Bersham, via Clawdd Coch or Llandrinio. The Forge closed in the 1750's. Upton Forge, much further upstream, was also served by small boats. Exact details are unknown, but in 1757 a sunken boat in the river was described as being 'made use of for the carriage of pigs and iron to and from Upton Forge'. This forge was still in operation in the 1820's but by that time it was being served by the Shrewsbury Canal.

In 1636 William Sandys began to improve the Warwickshire Avon and at the same time had permission to improve the River Teme as far upstream as Ludlow 'whereby the counties... may be better supplied with wood, iron, pit-coals, and other commodities which they now want'. There is no evidence that any work on this scheme was carried out although short sections were used occasionally by very small boats. Now the Teme, with its weirs and rapids, is the best white water canoeing river in the county.

At the end of the eighteenth century, despite the increased amount of traffic, the Severn was becoming more unreliable, mainly due to improved drainage and flood prevention schemes upstream of Shrewsbury and a general lack of maintenance. The opening of the Shrewsbury Canal in 1797 reduced the river traffic above Ironbridge but, overall, the national canal system actually helped to increase traffic on the rest of the river for a while. Ambitious schemes to canalize the river, or humbler ones at least to introduce proper weirs on its upper reaches, came to nothing.

The opening of the Severn Valley Railway in 1863 virtually meant the end of the river traffic. There had, in any case, been only one barge a week working to Shrewsbury since, the 1850's. The towpaths still belonged to the Trustees, who no longer had any income to maintain them. In the 1890's, a barge was still at work carrying roadstone from Belan Bank near Melverley to a wharf near Shrewsbury. Traditionally, the last working barge from the Ironbridge Gorge foundered after hitting Bridgnorth bridge in 1895. In 1899 a horse-drawn barge was hauled upstream from Gloucester to Shrewsbury and displayed in the town as a curiosity before being broken up for firewood.

Boats still use the Severn, and once again in increasing numbers as more and more people realise the delights of 'messing about on the river'. Rowing boats and canoes are by far the most common craft, with the occasional cabin cruiser and tripper boat. 'The building of Shrewsbury Weir as part of a flood prevention scheme in the early years of this century effectively split the river in two as only canoes could shoot or bypass it. Plans in the late 1950's to build a larger weir at Shelton were stopped after protests from many quarters, including a demonstration by a small armada of river craft. In the 1980's plans were drawn up for a scheme to resurrect the eighteenth century dream of an improved, navigable Severn. The construction of the many weirs and locks needed for this scheme would undoubtedly destroy the historic character and natural beauty of the river. The continuing opposition against the scheme has combined conservationists, landowners, anglers and canoeists and it seems very unlikely that it will ever go ahead.

This rather inaccurate engraving of the 1790's shows a tub-boat on the Donnington Wood Canal being towed past Lilleshall Abbey.

The Early Canals

The opening of the Bridgewater Canal near Manchester in 1761 heralded the start of the 'Canal Age', and the rapid expansion of a national canal network was a vital factor in the industrialisation of Britain in the late eighteenth and early nineteenth centuries, the era of the Industrial Revolution. Unlike the rivers, the canals could go virtually anywhere, crossing hills and valleys to provide vital transport links between raw materials, manufactories and markets. However, canals were certainly not a new invention.

Canals probably developed from the early irrigation systems of the ancient civilisations of the Middle East. By the tenth century AD the Chinese had developed the crucial pound-lock, an invention that had reached Holland by the fourteenth century. Canals were built in a series of long, level sections. Usually the highest level, the summit level, was the longest of all. Locks were used to get boats from one level to another and the most common type consisted of a brick or masonry chamber, the pound, with a gate at each end. One gate would be opened to allow the boat to enter the lock, and then be closed after it. Sluices would then be opened to raise or lower the water level in the pound. Once that was finished, the other gate would be opened and the boat would continue on its way. The earliest canals in Britain were probably the Caerdyke and Fossdyke, built by the Romans, but the first pound-locks in Britain appeared on the short Exeter Canal, opened in 1566.

The Bridgewater Canal took its name from the Duke of Bridgewater and was built to link coal mines at Worsley with the rapidly growing industrial town of Manchester nearby. The engineer was James Brindley but the Duke's land agent, John Gilbert, also had an important role in its construction. The Duke's brother-in-law was Lord Gower, who owned coal mines and limestone quarries in East Shropshire. His land agent was John Gilbert's brother, Thomas.

Given these family connections it is not surprising that the first canal in Shropshire was built by Lord Gower and the two Gilbert brothers, who formed the Earl Gower & Company in 1764. They planned a canal over private land between coal pits at Donnington Wood and a roadside wharf at Pave Lane on the Wolverhampton-Newport turnpike, with a branch canal from Hugh's Bridge to the limestone quarries at Lilleshall. There were 30 men at work by the start of February 1765, being paid from just 3½d (1.67p) to 12d (5p) per day, and the 5½ miles of the main line had been finished by the end of 1767.

As at Worsley, at least some of the seams at the mine were navigable, and boats could travel into the workings. The Donnington Wood main line was a level canal, fed by water from the mine drains and small streams along the route. It needed no locks, and was fairly easy to build. However, the level of the branch canal was 42 ft. 8 ins. below that of the main line, which at this point ran along a ridge of high land. The difference in level was too great to be solved by building locks. Instead, the branch canal was continued in a short tunnel into the ridge. Two parallel shafts were sunk alongside the main canal down to this tunnel, and cargoes were raised and lowered in the shafts in crates. As most of the traffic down the branch line was coal, full crates of coal were attached by a pulley system to lighter crates of limestone to be brought up from the branch line, and the weight of the falling coal helped raise the limestone.

Near to the northern end of the branch canal, at Wildmoor Bridge, a second branch ran eastwards to some limeworks, a coal wharf and Pitchcroft quarry. This branch descended 35 ft., but did so through seven small pound-locks. These were the only locks on the canal. The main traffic of the canal was always coal and limestone, with coal from the pits taken either to the wharf at Pave Lane for sale, or down the branch to fuel the limeworks supplying agricultural lime. Limestone not used in the limeworks was taken to the ironworks at Donnington Wood to be used as flux.

A restored tub-boat and ice-breaker on the Shropshire canal at Blists Hill.

The traffic was carried in small, 3 ton, wooden boats, less than 20 ft. long and 6 ft. 4 ins. wide, with a draught of about 1 ft. 6ins. These were the model for most of the craft used on the canal system of East Shropshire and became known as tub-boats. They were hauled by horses walking along the towpath, often controlled by a boy.

The name of the canal changed to that of the chief landowner in 1786 when Lord Gower was created Marquess of Stafford and again in 1833 when his son became the Duke of Sutherland. In 1802 the Marquess of Stafford had become the senior partner in what was to become the Lilleshall Company, a major industrial concern which leased most of the canal.

Despite the example, and apparent success, of the Donnington Wood canal, it was to be two decades before any significant attempts were made to build more canals in the county. This was not just due to a lack of interest or foresight. Lord Gower and Thomas Gilbert, for example, were key figures in the promotion of Britain's first trunk canal, the Trent & Mersey, authorised in 1766. In that same year a more ambitious, but abortive, scheme was put forward by Sir Richard Whitworth to link the rivers Severn, Trent and Weaver including the canalising of the River Tern near Atcham, and a canal along the Tern and Strine valleys through Newport to Great Bridgeford.

There were two small canal schemes in south Shropshire. In July 1778 an advertisement was placed in the 'Shrewsbury Chronicle' inviting tenders 'for making a navigable cut of the dimensions of six and a half feet in height and four feet in breadth for conveying the mines... to the mouth of the cut'. The location was Titterstone Clee, and the canal was to be driven a thousand yards into the hillside to the Gutter Works colliery. As well as taking small boats into the mines it was to act as a main drain, but there is no evidence to suggest that it was ever started.

To the east, two forges were built near to the west bank of the Severn at Eardington. The Upper Forge was probably built between 1777-8 and the Lower Forge shortly after, in 1782. An underground canal ran due east from the Upper Forge pond for some 750 yds. to a rock-cut basin by the side of the Lower Forge's riverside wharf. It was nine foot wide and appears to have been built to be used by small boats but details of such traffic are unknown. The Upper Forge closed in the 1820's and presumably the canal was disused after that date.

The Severn was clearly seen as capable of handling most of the traffic and in the still growing industrial area of East Shropshire the terrain was difficult for canal construction. The area was also well served by a fairly efficient and extensive waggonway system, built up over two centuries and linking most of the important mines and manufactories with the Severn and with each other.

CANAL MEETING.

NOTICE is hereby given, that a Meeting of the Subscribers to the proposed Canal from the Lime Works at or near Lilleshall, to join the Canal from the Trent to the Merfey, at or near Stone, with a Branch to or near to the Town of Market Drayton, will be held at the Red Lion Inn, in Newport, in the County of Salop, on Monday the 22d Day of January Instant.

January 8, 1798.

For every canal scheme that was actually started, there were many that never left the planning stage. The idea of an eastern extension from Lilleshall was still being mooted in the 1820's.
(Salopian Journal, 10th January 1798)

In the late eighteenth century, East Shropshire was undoubtedly one of the most industrially innovative areas in the world, and one of its most remarkable inhabitants was the ironmaster, William Reynolds of Ketley. He was enthusiastic about improving all aspects of transport in the area and aware of the economic advantages of doing so. By the time he had reached his late twenties, he had sufficient confidence in his own abilities, and sufficient capital, to put his ideas into practice. In 1787 he was involved in three small canal schemes and contemplating a far more ambitious one.

His father, Richard Reynolds, managed the Coalbrookdale Company as well as the iron works at Donnington Wood. In 1787 William proposed to build a short canal, two miles long, from newly discovered deposits of coal and ironstone at Wombridge to the western end of the Donnington Wood Canal. The Wombridge Canal was opened in the following year, and cost £1,640 to build. It was a tub-boat canal and on the same level as the Donnington Wood, with no need of locks. The one unusual feature of the canal is that it passed through a brick-lined tunnel near to Wombridge itself. A shallow cutting would have been cheaper to make and the reasons for the tunnel are unknown. It may simply have been built to placate a local landowner.

The first reference to the Coalbrookdale Navigation occurs in June 1787. Despite its name, it was started near to the Severn at what is now Coalport. The navigation seems to have been an ambitious attempt to provide an underground canal system, fed by mine drainage, linking the collieries around Blists Hill. After the tunnellers had dug about three hundred yards, they struck a rich source of natural bitumen. This provided an unexpected and profitable bonus and the subterranean navigation was abandoned. Instead, reservoirs were built to store the bitumen and in 1796 a plateway was built into the tunnel, then some thousand yards long. Bitumen continued to be taken until 1843 and the tunnel was still used for mine ventilation until the 1930's. The first part of this, the famous 'Tar Tunnel', is now open as a tourist attraction.

Although only one and a half miles long, the third canal, the most innovative of all, was built in partnership with his father. In January 1788 William Reynolds said in a letter that 'Indeed I have my hands full - we are making a canal from Oakengates to Ketley & have between 2 and 300 men at work upon it & ... I am head and subschemer, Engineer and Director'. The Ketley Canal linked coal and ironstone mines around Oakengates with the Coalbrookdale Company's Ketley works and was finished in the summer of 1788.

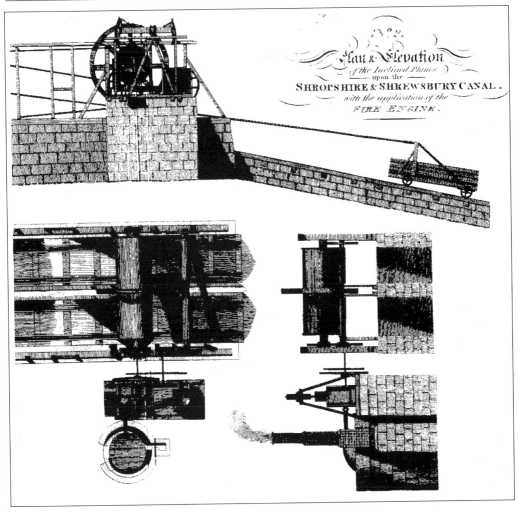

These diagrams of one of the inclined planes were drawn by W. Jones for Telford's section on canals written for Plymley's "A General View of the Agriculture of Shropshire" published in 1803.

The canal was built on the level to just east of the Ketley works, and ended on a ridge of high ground some 73 feet above them. The situation was similar to that encountered by the Gilberts, at Hugh's Bridge, but Reynold's solution was dramatically different. He adopted a device that had been used on the local waggonways since the middle of the century - the inclined plane.

Two parallel tracks were laid on a steep slope between the two levels. At the top of the incline, the canal ended in a pound-lock, with a sloping bottom, into which the tub-boats were floated. They were gently lowered onto a wheeled cradle as the water was emptied from the lock. The cradle was designed with a larger lower and small upper pair of wheels so that the tub-boat would remain reasonably horizontal as it was lowered down the plane. A connecting rope was coiled around a brake-drum at the head of the plane and linked to another cradle at the bottom. As the cradle with the full tub-boat began its descent on one track, it helped to haul the cradle with the empty one up the slope. The rate was controlled by a man operating a brake on the drum. At the bottom of the incline, the tub-boats were floated into a short stretch of canal leading into the works.

The benefits of the inclined plane were substantial. A whole 'staircase' of expensive pound-locks was not needed, the time taken by the tub-boats was reduced, and, perhaps more importantly, the system wasted very little water. At Ketley, in dry periods, a small steam engine pumped the water lost from the top lock back up from the bottom of the plane, A similar system had been used on the Tyrone Canal in Ireland in 1777 but was unsuccessful. Reynolds, however, could write to James Watt in 1789 that 'Our Inclined Plane answers my most sanguine expectations ... we have already let down more than forty boats per day each carrying 8 tons - in average about thirty boats daily and have not yet had an accident'. The rails used on the Ketley incline were not those of the wooden waggonways, but cast iron 'L' section plates. This was probably the first time these type of rails were used in the area but many of the older waggonways were soon to be rebuilt as horse-drawn 'plateways'. There is little doubt that Reynolds used the inclined plane at Ketley as an experiment to demonstrate to other local businessmen that great changes in height need not impede canal development. There is also little doubt that the Ketley Canal was, from the first, planned to be a branch canal for a much more ambitious project, the Shropshire Canal. Ironically, the Ketley Works were closed in 1816 and the canal abandoned by 1818.

The Shropshire Canal

Those shareholders lucky enough to have invested in
a profitable company were entitled to dividends.
(Salopian Journal, 10th October 1978)

Unlike the earlier canals in the county, built with private capital across private land for private traffic, the canal William Reynolds was planning from Donnington Wood to the Severn was to be built by a new public company set up by an Act of Parliament. The necessary finance came from the shareholders, who in turn expected dividends on their investment once the canal started to bring in money from the tolls paid by craft using it.

The Act 'for making and maintaining a navigable Canal from the Canal at Donnington Wood, in the county of Salop, to or near a Place called Southill Bank, and from thence by two several Branches, to communicate with the River Severn' was given the Royal Assent on the 11th June, 1788. It had an authorised capital of £50,000 and the major shareholders were connected with the local iron and coal industries. Richard Reynolds was the chief shareholder with £6,000 worth of shares, the ironmaster John Wilkinson had £5,500, the Marquess of Stafford £2,000 and William Reynolds £1,000. The shareholders elected a Committee which met for the first time on the 13th June 'At the house of Michael Scillitoe at the Bank, nr. Dawley, innkeeper'. John Loudon was appointed Engineer at a salary of £100 per annum.

The route went through difficult and hilly terrain, and would have been impossible without the use of inclined planes. The number of conventional pound-locks that would have been needed to cope with the change in levels would not only have been prohibitively expensive, but would also have required an enormous water supply. Work started at the north end of the main line in the summer of 1788 and one of the more unusual regulations to be enforced was that 'no sharpening of Tools... (was to) ... be paid for by the Company'.

The section at the foot of the Donnington Wood incline was built by the Donnington Wood company. This inclined plane had a rise of 120 ft. in 316 yds. up to the Shropshire's summit level. From there the canal ran through Wombridge to Snedshill, the junction with the Ketley Canal, and on southwards through Hollinswood to Southall Bank. There were three tunnels, a short one under Watling Street, and longer ones at Snedshill (279 yds. long) and Southall Bank (281 yds. long). These tunnels were 10 ft. wide at water level and 13 ft. high. For the most part, the canal was 16 ft. wide and 4 ft. 6 ins. deep, and the Committee decided that the boats using it should be 20 ft. long and 6 ft. 2 ins. wide, drawing less than 3 ft. when loaded.

The Aqueduct on the western branch of the Shropshire Canal still survives.
The local community which grew up nearby was named after it.

Southall Bank was the site of a temporary wharf, the carpenters' and blacksmiths' shops and the builders' store yards. At this point the canal divided into the 'two several Branches' mentioned in the Act, the Western branch heading for the Severn via Horsehay and Coalbrookdale, the Eastern heading for the river by the more direct route through Blists Hill.

Work on the main line went well and in December Loudon was ordered to start work on the Western branch. After crossing the Wellington to Bridgnorth road on a plain but elegant stone-faced aqueduct, it followed the contours of the land, looping north towards the Horsehay Works. The original proposal for a short branch canal to those works was abandoned in favour of a plateway. The canal then headed south and reached the top of Brierly Hill, overlooking Coalbrookdale.

An inclined plane at this point was to take traffic down to a portion of canal running along the east flank of Coalbrookdale southwards as far as the Rotunda on Lincoln Hill, from where a second inclined plane would run down to a short canal parallel to the river at Dale End. However the waggonway system through Coalbrookdale was well established and efficient and was being improved by the introduction of plateways. The construction of an expensive canal below Brierly Hill seemed inappropriate and was postponed in 1790 and abandoned two years later.

The problem of getting goods between the canal terminus and the Dale below still had to be overcome. In February 1790 the Coalbrookdale Company obtained permission to replace the proposed inclined plane with a tunnel and shaft system similar to that used on the Donnington Wood Canal at Hugh's Bridge. Two shafts, 120 ft. deep and 10 ft. in diameter, were sunk near to the ridge of the hill. The canal was extended into a four-bay terminus, the bays separated by three short piers. The two side piers each contained one of the shafts and above each shaft was a pulley mechanism. These were connected by a long rope wound around a large horizontal drum held in a solid frame on the central pier.

All the cargo taken by the tub boats on this branch was carried in special iron crates, four to each boat and each capable of carrying 2 tons of iron or coal. When one of these early container boats arrived at the dock, a large crane would unload a single crate and then move it across so that it could be attached to the hook of the pulley system above the adjacent shaft. Virtually all the traffic going down into the Dale consisted of coal and iron for the works and most of the traffic being taken from the Dale consisted of limestone for other ironworks so, as at Hugh's Bridge, the heavier 'down' cargoes helped lift the 'up' cargoes. At the bottom of the shafts, the crates were loaded or unloaded on or off specially designed trucks on a plateway running in a tunnel dug into the flank of the hill, described in 1801 as 'a huge subterraneous vault several hundred yards in Length'.

The self-acting system, which may have been working by July 1791, and certainly by October 1792, cost £2,742. Despite the expense, it proved to be inefficient and unreliable and in the Spring of 1793 broke down. It was altered so that the crates for the tub-boats were loaded directly onto plateway trucks and then pushed, two at a time, into a cage suspended above the shaft which was then lowered in the same way as the crates had been. At the bottom the trucks were pushed into a short siding until a train of six trucks was ready to be hauled down the Dale by horse power. The alterations did not help and in the autumn, the Coalbrookdale Company decided to replace the shafts with an inclined plane which was in operation by September 1794. The Brierly Hill incline did not carry boats, only plateway wagons carrying the crates from the tub-boats. As a great deal of traffic to and from Coalbrookdale was to Horsehay, only a mile or so along the canal, the Coalbrookdale Company obtained permission in 1800 to lay a plateway along the

The Hay Inclined Plane at the turn of the century

towpath to Horsehay wharf. This avoided the need to use the canal between the two points at all and this section, barely eight years old, was effectively abandoned.

Work on the Eastern branch was started in the summer of 1789. South of Southall Bank the longest incline, at Windmill Farm, descended 126 ft. in 600 yds. to the Cuckoo Oak. The canal then passed Madeley and Blists Hill before ending at the Hay Farm on a ridge high above the river Severn. The Hay Incline was by far the most spectacular of all, dropping 207 ft. in just 350 yds. to a stretch of canal running parallel to the Severn.

Loudon resigned in October 1789 and the position of Engineer, or 'General Inspector and Surveyor', was taken by Josiah Heatley in December. He in turn was sacked two months later and his replacement, James Pearcy, lasted less than a year before meeting the same fate. The post was eventually filled by the very capable Henry Williams, of Ketley.

By September 1790 the company was collecting tolls from traffic using the part of the canal at the summit level, and work on the three inclined planes was well underway. Despite the success of the incline on the Ketley Canal, the Committee had, at their first meeting, offered a reward of 50 guineas to 'that Person who shall discover... the best Means of raising and lowering heavy Weights from one navigation to another'. In October 1788 the prize was won jointly by their own engineer, John Loudon and Henry Williams.

'Schemer' Williams, was an influential figure in local canal matters and had probably been involved in the design of the Ketley incline. On the Shropshire inclines the top lock was replaced by a short back slope, to save water. Each incline had a double track of plateway laid upon it made up of flanged cast iron rails. 6 ft. long. 8 ins. wide, 2 ins. thick with a flange 3 ins. high, that were fixed to wooden sleepers. The track ran up and over the crest and down the back slope into the loading dock. The boat entered a dock at the top of the incline and was chained to one of two cradles, one running on each track. These were made of heavy baulks of wood reinforced with wrought iron, with front wheels 2 ft. 3 ins. in diameter and smaller rear wheels just 1 ft. 5 ins. in diameter, ensuring that the cradle held the boat level during the descent. In addition, a third pair of rear wheels, 2 ft. in diameter, were used on the back slope section for the same reason.

A stationary steam engine hauled the cradle up the back slope and out of the water, after which everything worked mainly through gravity as on the Ketley prototype. Most traffic on the Windmill Farm and Hay inclines was downwards, so that the steam engines were seldom needed to help in hauling up the cradle from the bottom, although they were designed to be able to do so. The situation on the Donnington Wood incline was different. As most traffic was being hauled upwards, the steam engine was needed virtually all the time. By October 1791 the incline at Donnington Wood was working. Those at Windmill Farm and the Hay were also in use, but were worked by horses until the Committee gave the go-ahead to install steam engines late in the following year.

When fully operational, the Windmill Farm incline could take six boats in either direction in one hour. Despite the lack of locks, reservoirs were needed to supply the canal and additional ones were still being built several years after it had opened throughout, in the latter part of 1791.

Tub-boats on the Eat Shropshire system were usually linked in trains of up to twenty, pulled by a single horse. This train is carrying coal, one of the principal cargoes of any canal.

The Shropshire Canal was soon paying dividends. Because the Western branch had stopped at Brierly Hill, the total construction cost of the canal was just £47,500 - less than the capital authorised in the Act. By the late 1790's the canal was carrying around 50,000 tons of coal alone each year, as well as considerable tonnages of iron. Virtually all the traffic was made up of short-trip working carrying iron, coal, limestone and sand between the industrial sites, apart from the coal and pig iron being exported through Coalport.

On the level stretches of canal the tub-boats were usually chained together in long 'boat trains', and it was not unusual for just one horse to haul twelve tub-boats carrying 60 tons of coal. Lighter cargoes, such as limestone, might even result in as many as twenty boats being hauled by a single horse. A man on the bank with a large pole had to ensure that the boats were kept in order and did not interfere with traffic coming in the opposite direction.

One major cause of dispute between the canal company and carriers was the extra payments charged on the inclined planes, as much as 3d (1.25p) per ton. There were continual arguments between the company and, in particular, the colliery owners. On several occasions, Williams was ordered to dismantle the steam engines and refuse access to the incline to anyone who would not pay the extra tolls. Whether this threat was ever carried out is not known, and the problem seems to have been resolved by the autumn of 1797.

The stretch of canal below the Hay Incline, running eastwards parallel to the river, had been built on 'a very rugged uncultivated bank, which scarcely produced even grass'. At the eastern end was a river lock to the Severn, with a drop of 22 ft. 10 ins. However, the small tub-boats using the Shropshire Canal were not suited to the more unpredictable waters of the Severn and no river barges from the river could use the canal's inclined planes. The river lock was quickly found to be another expensive mistake and was soon filled in.

Instead, short, miniature inclined planes were laid on the slope between the bottom section of canal and the wharves; these were all self-acting, as virtually all the cargoes were being shipped onto the river barges and trows, rather than coming onto the canal system. There was also a huge transhipment warehouse between the canal and the river. William Reynolds exploited the attraction of a good transport system and within a few years the new village of Coalport had two potteries, a chain works and a rope factory. In 1810 a new basin was dug to take 60 tub-boats and the wharves were extended.

One consequence of the success of the Shropshire Canal's inclined planes was the closure of the tunnel and shaft system at Hugh's Bridge on the Donnington Wood Canal. The replacement inclined plane, 123 yds. long, was in service by 1797 and was similar to that in use at Brierly Hill, in that plateway waggons rather than boat cradles were used on it. Plans to continue the line of the canal eastwards from either Pave Lane or Lilleshall to the Trent & Mersey Canal at Stone came to nothing.

The achievement of the Shropshire Canal was summed up later by Thomas Telford when he wrote that 'This canal, carried over high and rugged ground, along banks of slipping loam, over old coal mines and over where coal mines and iron stone are now actually worked under it, is satisfactory proof that there is scarcely any ground so difficult, but where, with proper exertions and care, a convenient water conveyance may always be obtained'.

Narrowboats could not use the inclines of the tub-boat system, and even between Wappenshall and Trench special 'narrow' narrowboats had to be built. the SUR&C had about twenty-four of these and one can be seen at the wharf below the Trench incline in 1921.

The Shrewsbury Canal

Shrewsbury, the county town and a major market for East Shropshire coal, was still reliant on the river Severn and on the poor road system. Much of its coal came from around Oakengates, several miles away from the Severn, and had to travel over fourteen miles along the Holyhead Road. By the 1790's it was said that 'this part of the road, from the constant succession of heavy coal carriages, had become almost impassable, notwithstanding that large sums of money were annually laid out upon the repairs of it'. The high cost of transporting the coal inevitably led to high prices and complaints that the townsfolk were 'so grievously imposed upon by the Jaggers and proprietors of coal teams'.

The success of the Shropshire Canal meant that raising the necessary capital for a canal to Shrewsbury was not difficult. It was promoted by some of those involved with the Shropshire Canal, including Richard and William Reynolds, John Wilkinson, John and Thomas Gilbert, and the Marquess of Stafford. These important industrialists were joined by major landowners along the route, including Lord Berwick of Attingham Park, John Corbett of Sundorne Castle, and John Charlton of Apley Castle.

The seventeen mile long route was first surveyed in 1792 by George Young of Worcester and the necessary Act setting up the Shrewsbury Canal Company was passed in the following year. From the start it was designed to be another tub-boat canal, taking boats of the same dimensions as those on the Shropshire Canal and its branches, rather than the larger and longer narrowboats already established on canals in other areas of the country.

The new company appointed Josiah Clowes as engineer in August 1793 but he died early in 1795 before the canal was finished. His replacement was Thomas Telford, part-time Surveyor of Public Works for Shropshire and recently appointed assistant to William Jessop on the Ellesmere Canal.

The company bought most of Reynold's Wombridge Canal, paying £840 for the easternmost 1 mile and 180 yds. to give them direct access to the Donnington Wood and Shropshire canals. The western end of the Wombridge Canal seems to have gone out of use after 1797. The new canal started at Trench, 75 ft. below the level of the Wombridge Canal, and an inclined plane was needed. At their first meeting, on the 6th July 1793, the Shrewsbury's Committee ordered 'That an Engine similar to the one at Donnington Wood be erected at the head of the intended Inclined Plane at Wombridge and that Mr. William Reynolds be requested to order the Engine from the Coalbrookdale Company and to forward the erection of it with all possible expedition'. The incline was 223 yds. long, and as most of the traffic was going down it in the Shrewsbury direction, the steam engine was only needed to haul the boat cradles over the lip at the head of the incline and up the back slope.

Although the canal did not have to cope with the severe gradients and unstable terrain tackled by the Shropshire Canal, it did have to overcome lesser changes in level, cross two small rivers, and somehow get through the high ground immediately to the east of Shrewsbury. Because much of the land along the route was prime agricultural land, its purchase price was higher than that in the coalfield area. The company also had to cope with the whims of certain landowners, such as Lord Berwick, who insisted that the towpath be on the opposite, or north, side of the canal to his home at Attingham as it passed through his estates.

Hadley Park lock on the Shrewsbury Canal, probably in the early nineteen hundreds, showing the unusual vertical gates used at the lower end of the chamber.

The canal needed eleven pound-locks, but the exact details of their original design are shrouded in some confusion. They were certainly unlike most of the other locks on the national canal network, being designed to take four tub-boats at a time. They were thus longer than usual, at 81 ft. long, but narrower, at just 6 ft. 7 ins. wide. Telford later described them as being specially built to take just one or two tub-boats at a time if necessary, using less water than four would, explaining that 'this is accomplished by having gates that are drawn up and down perpendicularly... and each lock has three gates, one of which divides the body of the lock'. This implied that just half the lock could be used if just one or two tub-boats were passing.

The locks appear to have been altered at an unknown date when the central gates were removed. If these had been installed, they must have been of the vertical lifting type described by Telford. Vertical, or 'guillotine', gates survived at the bottom of the locks, but the top gates were probably always of the more conventional swing-gate type.

The east portal of the Berwick Tunnel bears the date 1797. It was the longest tunnel in the county and if the canal had been built a few years later, a cutting would probably have been used instead.

The guillotine gates were operated by counterbalancing a suspended central weight, a wooden box full of stones, attached to chains running round an horizontal wooden axle supported by the gate frame. In 1840 the lock at Wheat Leasowes was altered and the old central weight system was replaced by one using 'a Counter Balance of Cast Iron in a well constructed at the back (i.e. side) of the Lock'. In the next few years all but three of the locks were modified in this way.

As with most canals of this date, the Shrewsbury tried, as far as possible, to follow the contours of the land to avoid drastic changes in level. When this was not possible, cuttings and shallow embankments were needed, or, as a final resort, a tunnel. Just to the east of Shrewsbury, Clowes had no option but to swing the canal southwards to avoid Haughmond Hill but this still required a tunnel between Berwick and the river ferry at Preston Boats. Originally called the Preston Tunnel, and later the Berwick, this was going to be 920 yds. long with cuttings at either end but at the start of 1795 it was decided to increase its length by 50 yds.

This was by far the longest canal tunnel in the county, but Clowes already had experience with a much longer tunnel when he worked on the Sapperton Tunnel on the Thames & Severn. The Berwick Tunnel had a slight bend in it which meant that it was impossible to see one end from the other. Most of the tunnel was just 10 ft. wide, but the entrances 'belled out' to appear wider. The portals were designed in a very simple, but suitably refined, style.

The tunnels on the Shropshire Canal, like all long tunnels on the national canal system up to this time, had no towpaths. Instead, the laborious process of 'legging' was needed where men lying flat on their backs on planks put their feet against the sides of the tunnel and 'walked' the boats through. Reynolds decided that a towpath was needed in this much longer tunnel and left the design to Clowes. The towpath, made only of planks on an open timber frame, was 3 ft. wide, leaving just 7 ft. of water for boats.

Despite the convenience for the boat crews, lack of maintenance meant that the towpath quickly fell into disrepair. It was removed towards the end of 1819 after which 'legging' was the order of the day with the towing horses having to walk over the line of the tunnel to pick up their charges at the other end. Despite its length and narrowness, there appear to have been no set rules for traffic using the tunnel laid down until 1838. The halfway point in the tunnel was marked by a white line and usually the train of tub-boats reaching it first had precedence over a train coming the other way. However, loaded boats always had precedence over empty ones no matter how far each train had travelled into the tunnel. As most traffic was going down to Shrewsbury, this meant that boats heading westwards had the right of way.

Apart from having the first major tunnel towpath in the country, the Shrewsbury Canal could also boast the first major iron aqueduct. Clowes had designed four masonry aqueducts. Two were quite small, single brick arches, one at Pimley, near Shrewsbury, over a small tributary of the Severn, and the other in the approach embankment to a larger aqueduct at Rodington. That aqueduct, of three arches, carried the canal over the River Roden. Work had started on a much longer aqueduct of the same basic design to carry the canal over the Tern at Longden-on-Tern. Fearful flooding in February 1795 wreaked havoc throughout the county and swept away many bridges over the Severn, and also damaged the incomplete aqueduct at Longden. The floods coincided with the death of Clowes and the appointment of Telford as his successor.

In the same month, Benjamin Outram had completed a small iron trough aqueduct on the Derby Canal and Telford would have known of this through his association with William Jessop, a business partner of Outram's. Even though Telford was, by training, a stonemason, he seems to have been working with Jessop on an idea to use iron in aqueducts on the Ellesmere Canal. On the 14th March, the Committee of the Shrewsbury company 'Ordered that an Iron Aqueduct be erected at Longden (agreeable to a plan approved by Mr. Telford) by Messrs William Reynolds & Company' and 'that such Aqueduct be erected at an expense not exceeding the sum of £2,000'. The idea was credited to the company's chairman, Thomas Eyton, but it seems very likely that Telford was keen to have the opportunity to see if an iron aqueduct could work.

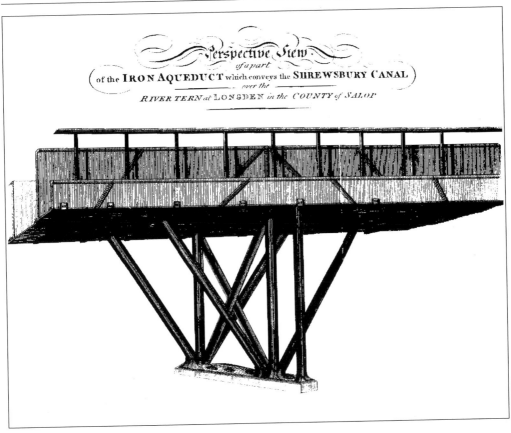

This early engraving of part of the Longden aqueduct, published in 1803,
shows its ungainly build and the separate framing of the towpath.

The design was almost certainly a joint effort by Telford and Reynolds, and the iron plates were cast at Reynolds' Ketley Works. The aqueduct was to be finished by September but seems to have taken slightly longer to complete as Reynolds was not fully paid until March 1796. However, at £1,750 it also cost less than anticipated. Clearly uncertain about the new technology, the Committee stipulated that Reynolds had to maintain the aqueduct for the first five years it was open. However, it seems to have given no trouble in that time.

The masonry arches and approach embankments designed by Clowes were repaired by Telford and only the central span of 62 yds. was of iron. The aqueduct was 7 ft. 6 ins. wide and 4 ft. 6 ins. deep, taking the canal 16 ft. above the river below. A separate trough alongside carried the towpath. It was certainly not a very attractive piece of industrial architecture, but it was the prototype of that astonishing symbol of the canal age - the Pontcysyllte aqueduct.

Longden aqueduct was still in water long after the canal was abandoned;
this photograph was taken in 1946.

The first portion of the canal to be finished, between the bottom of the Trench Incline and Long Lane Wharf, was open by the end of 1794. By March 1796 the canal had been extended past the new aqueduct at Longden where there was another public wharf, to Attingham. Here, the Berwick Wharf was named in honour of Lord Berwick. There is some topographical evidence to suggest that this wharf was originally going to be built at the end of a short branch canal, running south from the main line to the Holyhead Road at Atcham. which was started but then abandoned. The canal was finally open to Shrewsbury in November 1796, ending at a terminus just to the north of the castle.

The company laid down their rates at a General Assembly in October 1796. Coal and limestone were to be charged at 2d per ton per mile, but to encourage the development of limekilns along the canal, these goods would be charged at 1½d per ton if delivered to places within thirty yards of it. Iron and general goods were also charged at 2d per ton, and there was an additional charge of 1d per ton on the Trench Incline. These charges proved too excessive and were soon all reduced to 1d per ton until rising again a few years later.

In March 1797 Henry Williams was appointed 'Agent and General Superintendent' of the Shrewsbury Canal at a salary of £200 per annum and for the next forty years he was in effective control of the entire Shropshire tub-boat system. The Shrewsbury Canal, which had cost just under £65,000 to build, was quietly prosperous for some time, but ironically the cost of coal in Shrewsbury was not reduced.

This timeless view of a canalside wharf, bridge and crane has gone forever.
This was Uffington Wharf, near Shrewsbury, in the late 1930's
and now only the cottages remain.

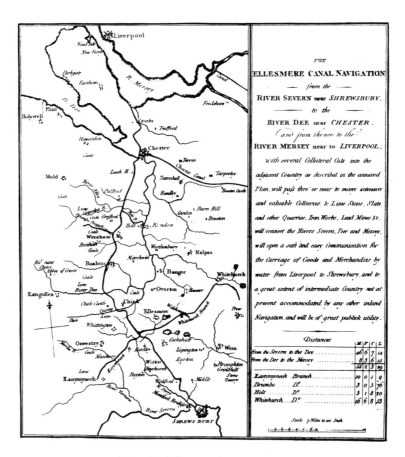

Map of the Ellesmere Canal circa 1793.

The Ellesmere Canal

Telford's experience of canal construction before taking on the Shrewsbury Canal had been restricted to one year working on an ambitious scheme to link the navigable rivers Severn, Dee and Mersey. Its origins lay in the need to improve the transport outlets of the growing iron making and coal mining areas of Denbighshire. The scheme was quickly caught up in the canal mania sweeping the country in the early 1790's after it was officially launched at Ellesmere in 1791.

The original route, surveyed by John Duncombe of Oswestry, ran from the Mersey at Netherpool across the Wirral to the Dee near Chester, and then southwards past Ellesmere, joining the Severn in Shrewsbury. Branches linked this main line with Ruabon, Llanymynech, Whitchurch and Wem. An alternative main line was proposed by another Shropshire engineer, William Turner of Whitchurch. It ran further to the east, using part of the almost moribund Chester Canal, a 'broad' navigation, capable of taking larger and wider barges than the normal narrow canals.

In 1792 the Committee appointed William Jessop, one of the leading canal engineers in the county, as advisor. He recommended a third, more ambitious route, running further west than Duncombe's, south from Chester to Wrexham and Ruabon and then on to Shrewsbury by way of Frankton and Weston Lullingfields. It required a tunnel near Ruabon over two and a half miles in length, one at Chirk nearly a mile long, and a third near to Weston Lullingfields, a mere quarter of a mile in length. Raising the canal up over three hundred feet from the flat Cheshire Plain to the edge of the Welsh mountains and then back down to the Severn Valley required dozens of locks. The crossing of the two steep-sided valleys of the Dee and the Ceiriog at Pontcysyllte and Chirk provided engineering problems of the highest magnitude. The estimated cost of this main line and of branches to Llanymynech, Holt and Whitchurch was almost £200,000. The new venture called itself the Ellesmere Canal Navigation, after the town nearest to the centre of the proposed system.

Despite the cost and the engineering difficulties, the general public, or rather those of the middle and upper classes with money to spare and the inclination to invest it, were keen to benefit from the potential profits that the canals could bring them. When the Ellesmere company opened the subscription for shares, there was pandemonium. In 1805 the then chairman, Rowland Hunt, described the event in the company's Report:-

'*The paroxysm of commercial ardour of the memorable tenth of September 1792 can never be forgotten by the writer, who had the honour to be left to defend the hill near the town of Ellesmere, which gives its name to the undertaking, from the excessive intrusion of too ardent speculation; the books were opened about noon, and ere sun set near a million of money was confided to the care of the Committee'.*

The sheer cost of the 'western line' gave temporary impetus to a rival 'eastern line' scheme, supported by the Chester Canal, backing Turner's route. However, at the start of 1793 this renegade group rejoined the main body, which obtained its Act on the 30th April 1793, and an authorised capital of £400,000. Jessop was appointed Engineer, with Duncombe and Turner as his assistants. In October the Committee appointed Telford, then with no experience of canal building, as 'General Agent, Surveyor, Engineer, Architect, and Overlooker of the Works' at £300 per annum. He was clearly junior to Jessop but had authority over both Duncombe and Turner.

The canal was very different in scope and design to the tub-boat canals of East Shropshire. Originally, it was seen as a major new trunk route linking the three important river navigations, and its locks and bridges were to be wide enough to take river barges. The cost was quickly seen as too great, and only the Wirral section was built as a 'broad' canal, capable of taking barges up to 14 ft. 6 ins. wide. The rest of the line was built as a 'narrow' canal, the locks capable of taking barges just less than seven foot wide but nearly seventy foot long. These aptly named 'narrowboats' were already in use throughout the country's canals.

The engineering problems of the northern portion of the main line were to cause many difficulties, result in many changes of route and in several new Acts. Rather than build the whole canal at once, the company decided to concentrate initially on those portions that could bring in revenue and the Wirral section was open by the summer of 1795. Netherpool itself was renamed Ellesmere Port.

Early in 1794 work started on the branch to Llanymynech, which left the main line below Frankton Locks, and a short

ELLESMERE CANAL NAVIGATION.
NOTICE IS HEREBY GIVEN,

THAT the Committee of the PROPRIETORS of the ELLESMERE CANAL NAVIGATION have this Day ordered that a Call of Five Pounds per Cent. shall be made upon the several Subscribers to and Proprietors of the said Navigation, in Proportion to their Shares and Subscriptions therein; and that Two Pounds and Ten Shillings per Cent. in Part of such Call, shall be paid on or before the Thirteenth Day of December next; and that the further Sum of Two Pounds and Ten Shillings per Cent, residue of the said Call, shall be paid on or before the Twelfth Day of February next to Messrs. EYTON, REYNOLDS, and WILKINSON, Bankers, in Shrewsbury, Treasurers to this Concern; Messrs. ROBARTS, CURTIS, WERE, and Co. Bankers, in London; or Messrs. BOULTBEE, MANSFIELD, and Co. Bankers, in Leicester; or Messrs. LLOYD and Co. Bankers, in Birmingham; to the Account of the said Messrs. Eyton, Reynolds, and Wilkinson, whereof this Notice is given, pursuant to the Directions of the Act for making the said Canal, by   CHARLES POTTS,
Clerk to the said Committee.
Chester, 29th October, 1794.

Most canals were financed by shareholders who invested in the company in order to make a profit. As the work progressed, the shareholders were called on to pay up. (Salopian Journal, 10th January 1795)

section of the main line itself running south-eastwards, from Frankton to a wharf at Hordley. The completion of the Llanymynech branch meant that the important limestone quarries in that area could be reached. Apart from a small masonry aqueduct over the River Perry and three locks at Aston, the eleven mile branch presented few engineering difficulties and was open by the autumn of 1796.

The Rev. John Lloyd, one of the original Committee members, persuaded the company to deviate from the authorised line a few hundred yards west of the Perry aqueduct to bring the canal nearer to his house, Woodhouse, near Rednal. Part of the original line had already been built and seems to have been left in water. The diversion was in turn abandoned, probably soon after 1800, and the original line finished.

After crossing the Welsh border at Llanymynech the branch ended in an end-on junction at Carreghofa with the Montgomeryshire Canal. This had originally been proposed as an extension to the Llanymynech branch but was eventually built and operated by a separate company which obtained an Act in March 1794 to build a canal from Carreghofa to Newtown. The junction at Carreghofa was open in the summer of 1797 and the main line of the Montgomeryshire as far as Garthmyl, together with a branch canal to Guilsfield, were ready by the autumn. Shortage of money and severe engineering problems meant that the rest of the line to Newtown was not open until 1819. This portion was built by a virtually separate company, which became known as the Western Branch as distinct from the older Eastern Branch, and there were endless disputes between these erstwhile allies for many years.

On the Ellesmere's main line, work started on the portion between Frankton and Pontcysyllte, even though the problems of crossing the Dee and Ceiriog valleys had yet to be resolved. The height of the summit level of the canal meant that the aqueducts required would have to be

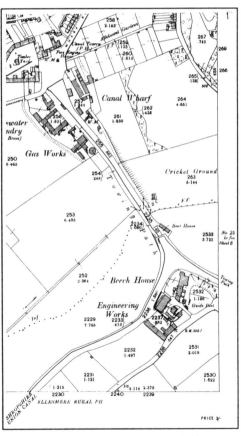

The Ellesmere branch on a map of 1901. Beech House was the headquarters of the SUR&C and their maintenance depot was the Engineering Works alongside. A dairy later took the place of the Bridgewater Foundry and the Gas Works.

exceedingly high, 125 ft. above the river in the case of Pontcysyllte, and thus exceedingly expensive. In 1794 the company wavered and accepted a plan for more locks and lower aqueducts but no work had been done on them by July of the following year when Jessop recommended to the Committee 'an Iron Aqueduct at the full height originally intended' at Pontcysyllte.

Telford later claimed that it was his idea to build the aqueduct in iron, and although this has been disputed, it is generally accepted that he designed it. Despite its vastly different scale, in principle Pontcysyllte was little different from Longden, consisting of an iron trough over a thousand feet long supported on 19 masonry piers of the highest quality, approached by a massive embankment on the southern side of the valley. It cost £47,018 - about the same as the whole of the Shropshire Canal. The company realised that the aqueduct was going to take time and money to complete, and that in the meantime they needed revenue. Work on the masonry piers, started in 1795, was stopped at the beginning of 1796 and work on the Chirk aqueduct was started instead.

The Ceiriog marks the boundary between Shropshire and Wales. Jessop had also recommended an iron aqueduct to cross this valley, suggesting that its comparative lightness of design would 'instead of an obstruction... be a romantic feature in the view' and accurately predicted that this would persuade a recalcitrant landowner to allow it to be built at Chirk instead of slightly upstream at Pontfaen. However, it was not built to the same design as that at Pontcysyllte and in many ways was a compromise between the old and the new technologies. Masonry aqueducts had to be very solid to cope with their own weight, the weight of the water in the canal, and the puddled clay lining the canal to make it leak-proof At Chirk, the conventional puddling was abandoned in favour of flat cast iron plates lining the waterway and also acting as a continuous structural tie, both laterally and longitudinally, for the masonry. Telford himself wrote that 'The sides of the canal were made waterproof by ashlar masonry with hard, burnt bricks laid in Parker's Cement'. The stonework no longer had to be completely solid, saving both weight and cost, and the ten arches between the piers were virtually hollow. It took five years to build, was 600 ft. long and 70 ft. high, cost nearly £21,000, and was, briefly, the longest in the country.

In the meantime, work was started on the section southwards from Hordley Wharf to Weston Wharf, which boasted four lime kilns, stables, a weighing machine, a clerk's house, and a public house. The canal was carried on for a further half mile in anticipation of the final link to Shrewsbury, ending just to the north of the proposed tunnel.

After negotiations with the Chester Canal, the idea of the old 'eastern line' was revived by the extension of the Whitchurch branch eastwards to the Chester Canal near Nantwich, and a map was published showing the Ellesmere system as a giant 'X', with waterways radiating from Frankton Junction to the Mersey, the Chester Canal, the Severn, and, via the Montgomeryshire Canal, to the heart of mid-Wales. Frankton had the potential to become a canal junction of some stature but was to remain

Chirk Aqueduct at 200 ft. long was the longest aqueduct in the country at the time it was built.

The locks at Frankton were looking decidedly derelict in the 1950's but are now, happily, restored.

a hamlet. There were really two junctions, with the locks (two standard and one 'staircase', effectively two locks in one) on the link between them. Above the locks the Whitchurch branch left the main line heading east, and below them, the Llanymynech branch headed westwards.

By 1797 the main line was open between the south end of Chirk aqueduct and Weston Lullingfields, the Llanymynech branch was completed, and work had started on the Whitchurch branch. All seemed to be going well, but the company was soon to meet severe problems. The opening of the Shrewsbury Canal meant that East Shropshire coal prices would undercut those of Chirk and Ruabon and work on the line south of Weston was first postponed and later abandoned. At the opposite end of the main line the enormous expense of the tunnels and locks needed to reach Chester were beginning to cause anxiety and in 1800, Jessop wrote 'It is wholly inadvisable to execute a canal between Pontcysyllte and Chester' because of the competition from horse-drawn railways from the collieries to the Dee. He suggested that the canal company build a railway and convert the proposed aqueduct at Pontcysyllte to a railway viaduct, thus saving over £8,000. That advice was ignored and the aqueduct was finished, but the canal to the north was never built.

Chirk aqueduct was finished by the autumn of 1801 and the canal had reached the south side of the Dee by the following summer, although Pontcysyllte was not open until November 1805. The abandonment of the line to the north, which included the canal's summit level, created an acute water supply problem solved by the construction of a navigable feeder, opened in 1808, fed from a weir across the Dee at Llantisilio and running past Llangollen to the north end of Pontcysyllte.

Progress on the Whitchurch branch was slow, partly because of engineering difficulties presented by the crossing of Whixall Moss, partly because of the difficulty of water supply, but mostly because money was no longer in abundance. By 1804 only twelve miles had been finished, but the twenty-nine miles to Hurleston Junction were open by the end of the following year. Whitchurch itself had been bypassed by the new route, but a branch was built from Grindley Brook and opened as far as Sherryman's Bridge in July 1808. There were problems with the marshy site, its owner, and the fact that it was still outside the town. The Earl of Bridgwater, however, demolished warehouses nearer the centre of Whitchurch which allowed the canal to be extended to a more convenient terminus by 1811.

Another branch left the Whitchurch line at Whixall Moss, running eastwards to Prees Heath on the main road between Market Drayton and Wellington. Edstaston Wharf was to be halfway along the branch and served nearby Wem. It had three wharves, warehouses, weighing machines, a winding hole (a triangular inlet for turning narrowboats), and two ale houses. Only the first four miles were built by 1806, ending at Quina Brook on the Wem to Whitchurch road where there was a long wharf, capable of taking four narrowboats, five limekilns, a warehouse, weighing machine, stables, winding hole, and crane. The rest of the branch remained unfinished.

The extension to the Chester Canal did at last unite the two isolated portions of the Ellesmere's system and also provided belated access to the Dee and the Mersey. But instead of being a transport link of national importance, the canal became an important part of the local transport system only, particularly for agricultural traffic. The fortunes of the Ellesmere and the Chester Canals had become so obviously linked that it was almost inevitable that the two concerns merged on the 1st July 1813 to become a new company, the Ellesmere & Chester Canal.

A wooden lift bridge at Whixall on the Prees Branch of the Ellesmere Canal.
These were designed to be cheaper than masonry ones.

The Leominster Canal

Despite never achieving its ambitious aims, despite never being finished and despite never being particularly profitable, the Ellesmere Canal eventually became a qualified success. That certainly could not be said for another contemporary product of the canal mania, running along the southern boundary of Shropshire.

The agricultural areas of south Shropshire and north Herefordshire both suffered from poor transport facilities which limited landowners from capitalising on the improvements in farming brought about in the latter part of the eighteenth century. Earlier attempts to make the river Teme navigable had been unsuccessful. Acts had been passed to make the river Lugg navigable in 1674, 1685 and 1727 and although locks had been built following the last Act, navigation from its confluence with the navigable Wye near Hereford upstream to Leominster had been, at best, erratic.

There had been outline schemes for a canal to link Ludlow with the Severn at Bridgnorth, and an ambitious scheme in 1777 to link Hereford with the Severn at Areley Kings, on the opposite bank of the river to the new canal port of Stourport. This idea was revived in 1789 and Thomas Dadford surveyed a route from Leominster which ran north to Wooferton and then westwards along the Teme valley. Criss-crossing the Shropshire border it passed Tenbury Wells before cutting through the hills west of Pensax to reach the Severn opposite Stourport. By April 1790 the route had been extended westwards from Leominster, so that the proposed canal had a total length of 46 miles through a purely agricultural region. Engineering difficulties included four tunnels, the longest being no less than 3,850 yds. at Pensax (which would then have been one of the longest in Britain), an aqueduct over the Teme just east of Wooferton, and a series of locks at the eastern end of the route taking the canal down 207 ft. to a basin by the Severn.

Before the scheme went to Parliament, it had been extended westwards to the limestone quarries and farmlands around Kington, and it was the Kington & Leominster Canal Company that obtained its Act in 1791 with an authorisation to raise a capital of £150,000. Dadford was appointed Engineer. Most of the envisaged traffic to the Severn was to be agricultural - lime, grain, flour, timber, leather, hops, cider and perry. In addition it was hoped that there would be a great deal of general traffic passing through the canal en route to Wales from all parts of England. The only important non-agricultural traffic locally, apart from some quarry traffic, was to be coal from Sir Walter Blount's pits near Mamble, which was to be supplemented by imported coal from the Midlands.

The canal mania was at its height and, at first, raising the money presented no difficulties and there were even serious proposals to link the Leominster Canal with others. The idea of a canal link from Leominster to Hereford was revived and an even more ambitious scheme was actually surveyed for a canal from Wooferton through Ludlow and Bishop's Castle to join the Montgomeryshire Canal near to Garthmyl. This would have been 41 miles long and cost an estimated £140,000. Neither scheme left the drawing board.

Work on the Leominster Canal seems to have been concentrated on the section running westwards from Southnet (then called Sousnant or Sousnett) Wharf, between Marlbrook and Mamble, presumably to enable Sir William Blount to export his coal as soon as possible, especially as he was one of the principal promoters of the canal. The company's headquarters were in the Wharf House, a fine Georgian brick building with a bowed front and large vaulted storerooms.

The rather fine Wharf House at Southnet Wharf on the Leominster Canal, just inside Shropshire, is a reminder of that company's ambitions.

The canal hugged the side of the Teme valley and an impressive aqueduct was needed to carry the line 40 ft. above the diminutive Rea brook near Newnham Bridge. This consisted of a single arch with a 45 ft. span, built entirely with bricks made on the site using the local clay, and Blount's coal. The construction was slightly unusual, with the canal taken in a brick-lined trough surrounded by puddled clay. It was reputed to be the largest single brick span of its time. A longer three-arched aqueduct, of brick and stone, crossed the Teme near Little Hereford and Brimfield. Work also started, at an unknown date, on a second aqueduct over the Lugg further upstream near Kingsland but this was quickly abandoned.

By the start of 1793 the short hundred yard tunnel at Newnham Bridge had been completed and work on the canal was going well. In May a barge called the 'Royal George' was launched at Tenbury Wharf and in October 1794 it was reported that 'the first boat's loading of coal', upon the Leominster Canal, which was from Sir William Blount's mines, arrived at Tenbury, and by his order was distributed among the poor of that place'. The canal, including 'the grand aqueduct' over the Teme, was actually opened between

Sousnant and Wooferton wharves and the celebrations were accompanied by the 'Ringing of bells, firing of canon, (and) roasting of sheep'. Wooferton Wharf boasted a basin and a warehouse, just to the west of the main Ludlow-Leominster road and not far from the Salway Arms.

This was to be the high point in the canal's history and the company was soon beset with problems. Between Wooferton and Leominster was another short tunnel, Putnal Fields, some three hundred and thirty yards long. Delays in its completion meant that it was still not ready by the end of 1795 even though the canal had been extended southwards from Wooferton to a temporary wharf at its northern portal. At the other end of the completed line the Southnet Tunnel, 1,254 yds. long, had been finished and work was well underway on a few hundred yards of canal further to the east of it. The finished portion of canal had not been extended eastwards into the tunnel, which remained unwatered. This was probably just as well for part of this brand new but unused tunnel collapsed a few hundred yards in from its east portal, giving rise to a legend that some of the workmen, and even a narrowboat, were entombed inside it.

In desperation the canal company called in the highly respected engineer, John Rennie, to inspect the works. He was not impressed. He criticised the design of the tunnels and the quality of their construction and also reported that the foundations of the Teme aqueduct and another one nearby, over the Rea brook, were insufficient. Undoubtedly part of the problem was a lack of supervision by Dadford of the contractors, especially as he was also working on the Monmouthshire Canal from 1792 onwards.

Eventually Putnal Fields tunnel 'which... long baffled the skill of the miners' was finished in the summer of 1796 and the canal was opened almost as far as Leominster by the end of the year. In fact, the temporary Leominster Wharf was built about a mile to the east of the town, on the Ludlow road, where an existing building was incorporated into the Wharf House. Just over eighteen miles of the proposed forty-six miles had been completed. The ill-fated Southnet Tunnel was left unrepaired and abandoned, and a short stretch of canal to the east of it, near Dumbleton Farm, was left unfinished, along with another short stretch to the west of the abandoned Kingsland aqueduct. Thomas Jenkins, the unfortunate tunnel contractor, left to attempt another long tunnel on the luckless Salisbury & Southampton Canal where he met with as little success as before.

Despite a second Act in 1796 to raise more funds, and a ceremonial sod-cutting by the side of the Severn in June 1797, the Leominster Canal was never to be finished and never actually to reach even Leominster itself. The canal mania was over and all the money had been spent.

The realisation that finishing the canal was impossible led to an alternate scheme in 1803 which envisaged building plateways along the line of the uncompleted sections of the canal. Plateways were already in use to connect the Mamble collieries with the canal.

Throughout the county there are reminders of long lost waterways. This old bridge
crosses the line of the Shrewsbury Canal near Rodington.

The new scheme was proposed by the engineer John Hodgkinson who had been trained by
one of the pioneers of long-distance plateways, Benjamin Outram. Hodgkinson was then
involved with several plateways in South Wales and his eminently practical idea was
accepted by the company and another Act authorising it was passed in August.

The route of the plateway from the Southnet Tunnel, which was to be repaired, was
surveyed and it is possible that some work was actually carried out. However, the
confidence of the shareholders in the company had been somewhat battered by its
indifferent performance and very little money was raised. The small revenue from the
cargo tolls was needed for basic maintenance and to pay off the interest on its debts and
there was simply none left to finance the plateways. As late as 1833 the scheme was
revived and in the following year the company paid John Raistrick to survey a route from
the Rea aqueduct to the Severn. Again, nothing came of the proposals and the canal was
to remain unfinished, unprofitable and totally isolated for the rest of its short existence.

Queens Head bridge had to be strengthened several times after 1902, the date of this drawing, to cope with the increasing road traffic on the A5, and was finally demolished after the Llanymynech branch was closed.

The Last Fling

By the early years of the nineteenth century the canal mania was over, leaving canals such as the Ellesmere and the Leominster unfinished. Even the more successful canals were soon to face the competition of the steam railways, although Shropshire was one of the last counties in England to 'hear the snort of the iron horse'. Until then the main competition to the county's canals, outside the East Shropshire area, was the road system, radically improved mainly because of the creation of turnpike trusts. The most important road in the county, the early nineteenth century equivalent of a motorway, was the London to Holyhead road, rebuilt by Thomas Telford between 1815 and 1830.

Despite his inventive and innovative approach to civil engineering and his tremendous achievements in canal, road and bridge building, Telford seemed to have little faith in the new-fangled railways. He thought they were being promoted in the late 1820's not to improve transport but as a ploy by vested interests. 'As the price of iron was depressed', he wrote, 'the ironmasters, to promote the consumption of that material, encouraged the construction of railways in sundry directions, the most important of which was a proposed line from Liverpool, through Birmingham, to London'.

This railway had been put forward in 1824 but Telford supported a rival canal scheme proposed by the prosperous Birmingham Canal company. The main waterway link between Birmingham and Liverpool had been the Trent & Mersey Canal, a rather roundabout route. The much more direct Birmingham & Liverpool Junction Canal was to run from Autherly Junction, on the Staffordshire & Worcestershire Canal not far from its junction with the Birmingham Canal, through Market Drayton to Nantwich where it would meet the former Chester Canal. By using the Ellesmere & Chester route through Chester and across the Wirral to Ellesmere Port, barges from Birmingham could reach the Mersey. The distance by water from Birmingham to Liverpool was considerably reduced.

The new company obtained the necessary Act in May 1826, the year after the opening of the Stockton & Darlington Railway. In the same session of Parliament, the Liverpool & Manchester Railway Act was also passed, heralding the real start of the 'Railway Age' and marking the beginning of the long drawn out decline of the canals. The authorised capital of the B&LJ was £400,000 (with a reserve of an additional £100,000 if necessary), and the engineer was Telford. He designed a canal that would directly challenge the railways, and benefit from the lessons learned from his canal and road building exploits.
In the eighteenth century few canals had been built with speed in mind. Instead they had followed the contours of the land as much as possible to prevent the need for too many

locks or engineering works. Speed, however, was one of the obvious attractions of the new railways; even the 30 mph available by 1830 was considered to be an amazing advance on the fastest of horse-drawn barges.

Using all his engineering skills and experience, Telford made his last canal run as straight as possible, all sharp corners eliminated and contours virtually ignored. This was achieved at some expense, by digging deep cuttings and building high embankments. He utilised the cut-and-fill method later used by the railways, in which material from cuttings was used to make the embankments. Locks were kept to a minimum and usually grouped together in flights. Of the 28 locks along the 40 mile long main line, 15 were grouped in one long flight at Audlem, just over the Shropshire border in Cheshire. Most of the others were in two five lock flights to the north and south of Market Drayton, at Adderley and Tyrley.

Large reservoirs were built to ensure an adequate water supply that did not have to rely too much on tapping small streams along the route. The price of this advanced engineering was high, the main line costing £16,000 per mile compared with just £7,241 per mile for the Western Branch of the Montgomeryshire Canal finished just a few years earlier.

One of the most spectacular stretches of the canal is undoubtedly the southern approach to Market Drayton. Woodseaves Cutting, cut out of the sandstone, is nearly a hundred feet deep in places and can be damp and gloomy. It is crossed by two small farm bridges that soar high above the canal, giving them an undeserved impression of grandeur. The cuttings were to cause problems to an ageing and ailing Telford, being too steep sided and subject to constant landslips. Far more trouble was caused by the embankments, and particularly that at Shelmore, just over the border in Staffordshire, and known as 'The Great Bank'. Another engineer was called in to deputise for Telford during his illness and although William Cubitt managed to solve the problem with the cuttings by reducing the angle of their sides, he too struggled with the 'Bank'. It took six years to build and delayed the opening of the canal until 1835, the year after Telford's death. By then, the company had exceeded its authorised capital and had been forced to obtain a further loan from the Exchequer. In all, the Birmingham & Liverpool Junction had cost in the region of £800,000, but that included the construction of a very important branch canal.

The Shropshire tub-boat canal network had remained isolated from the rest of the national canal network, and any traffic from the area that was taken by inland navigation to other parts of the country had to go the long roundabout route via Stourport, often being transhipped from tub-boat to river barge, and from river barge to narrowboat. The construction of a new trunk canal within a few miles of the nearest tub-boat canal altered matters considerably.

Horse-drawn narrowboats plodding through steep-sided Woodseaves Cutting on the main line of the Shropshire Union Canal, the former B&LJ, linking the Midlands and Merseyside.

The Birmingham & Liverpool Junction committee were also anxious to obtain traffic for their canal and initially approached the Lilleshall Company, lessees of the Donnington Wood Canal, soon after their Act had been passed, with proposals for a link between Gnosall Heath and Pave Lane. These were rejected and the B&LJ then approached the Shrewsbury Canal company instead, proposing a branch from Norbury passing through Newport to a junction with the Shrewsbury at Wappenshall. At a General Assembly of the Shrewsbury Canal held at the Raven Hotel, Shrewsbury, in October 1826, the company agreed to the B&LJ's scheme and the necessary Act was passed in the following year.

For various financial reasons, work on the branch was delayed for a few years but it was finished on the 12th January 1832, a few weeks before the main line. For the first time, Shropshire had a direct link to the Midlands canal network. The branch was just over ten miles long and had twenty-three locks, of which no less than seventeen were in a flight near to Norbury Junction. It was built to the same dimensions and in the same ambitious style as the rest of the main line.

There was one obvious problem. The craft on the B&LJ were narrowboats, and if they were to use any sections of the tub-boat system, alterations would have to be made. It was quickly apparent that rebuilding any of the inclined planes to enable them to take 70 ft. long narrowboats would be prohibitively expensive, and that it would only be the Shrewsbury Canal that could be changed.

In March 1831 the long-serving Henry Williams reported to the company's committee that altering the locks and bridges between Wappenshall and Shrewsbury would cost £1,000 and that the additional tonnage envisaged would more than pay for the work. By October, six bridges had been rebuilt and two others were being altered. The two locks at Eyton were widened to 7 ft. 4 ins.

However, narrowboats do not seem to have been allowed on the Shrewsbury for some time, for in April 1834 Williams was ordered to procure a 'long boat', laden with 20 tons of cargo, to see if it could safely pass trains of tub-boats, and, most importantly of all, negotiate the Berwick tunnel. The experiment was a success and narrowboats could at last reach Shrewsbury. This meant that the county town had a new outlet for dairy products brought in from the surrounding areas, which led to the building of the Butter Market in 1835 at Shrewsbury Wharf.

The proposals to widen the locks and bridges on the section south of Wappenshall to the foot of the Trench Incline were initially postponed and then, in October 1836, effectively abandoned. Most of the cargoes of the East Shropshire coalfield - in particular coal, iron, iron goods, and bricks - originated above the incline and had to be loaded into tub-boats initially anyway. Although some tub-boats did venture along the Newport branch and even, on occasion, onto the main line of the B&LJ, most stopped at Wappenshall where cargoes were transhipped into narrowboats. There seemed to be little

As late as 1965 there was still one lengthsman employed by the British Waterways Board on the old Shrewsbury Canal. Malcolm Edwards lived on the 24ft. maintenance boat, seen here at Berwick just after negotiating the tunnel.

The warehouse and roving bridge at Wappenshall Junction, where the tub-boat and narrowboat systems met, photographed in 1967. Fortunately both have survived.

point in improving the canal south to Trench, although later some special 'narrow narrow' boats (later called 'Shroppies') were built to use this section, being just 6 ft. 4 ins. wide.

Wappenshall became an important junction between the tub-boat and narrow-boat systems. As well as dealing with goods being exported from the coalfield area, it dealt with a very wide range of imported consumer goods brought in by narrowboat. By no means all of its cargo came by canal, and the road to the wharf became one of the busiest in the county. Wappenshall prospered and its capacity was extended by the building of a new warehouse a few years after it was opened. The canal companies did not benefit directly from any wharfage tolls, however, because the Duke of Sutherland had retained ownership of the wharf.

Two branch canals had also been authorised from the Newport Branch in the Act. One was a short link running from just west of Newport to the village of Edgmond, but this was never built. The second was to be a longer line, leaving the Newport Branch in the Weald Moors and running south to the Duke's varied enterprises around Donnington and Lilleshall. It would have had seven locks but a proviso in the Act allowed it to be replaced in part or full by a tramway. A short section, just under a mile long, was built and ended in a new wharf, also owned by the Duke, at Lubstree; the branch became known as the Humber Arm and opened in May 1844 becoming an important exporter of coal and pig iron.

The B&LJ's through route to the Mersey had only been possible because of the co-operation of the Ellesmere & Chester company, who in turn were given access from their system to the Midlands and the rest of the canal network. They had also managed to build a new branch canal of their own, authorised in 1827 and opened in 1833, linking the Chester Canal just north of Nantwich with a short branch of the Trent & Mersey near Middlewich. This short cut reduced the distances to Manchester considerably. The construction costs of Telford's trunk canal had virtually bankrupted the B&LJ and within a few years of opening they were considering a merger with the Ellesmere company. In May 1845 the two companies obtained their amalgamation Act, but the new enlarged company, still called the Ellesmere & Chester, was to be very short lived.

In contrast with the busy lock scene at Newport, this undated photograph shows the same canal nearby becoming derelict later in the century after most of the traffic had ceased.

Decline and Fall

1845, the year when the county's largest, the Ellesmere & Chester, and newest, the Birmingham and Liverpool Junction, canal companies amalgamated, marked the start of the railway mania. Even in rural Shropshire new companies were being set up to promote and hopefully to build railways connecting all the major towns and industries. Only too conscious of the threat to their livelihood, the proprietors of the Ellesmere & Chester company had been discussing how to cope with the new and more efficient transport offered by the railways. With the encouragement of their engineer, W.A. Provis, they eventually came to the conclusion that the only way to survive was to build railways themselves, using their one principle asset - ownership of many existing routes which, at comparatively little expense, could be converted from canals to railways.

At the same time, negotiations were underway with other canal companies in the county in an attempt to create an even larger undertaking and by the autumn of 1845 the Shropshire Union of Railways & Canals had been formed, although it did not receive its enabling Act until the following year. The SUR&C included the Ellesmere and Chester and the Shrewsbury Canal, but negotiations with the Shropshire Canal were protracted and eventually that company was leased for 21 years in 1849. In the meantime, the SUR&C had incorporated the Eastern Branch of the Montgomeryshire canal in 1847, the Western Branch following in 1850. The SUR&C had itself quickly lost its independence, being leased by the powerful London & North Western Railway in 1847.

The L&NWR's main reason for taking the canal company over was to prevent it from converting its canals to railways and thus becoming a competitor. The SUR&C were allowed to build one line, from Shrewsbury to Stafford, but all their other schemes were postponed indefinitely and they were to remain essentially a canal company to the end. They did try and persuade the L&NWR to allow them to revive their railway ambitions, even as late as the resurgence of railway fever in the early 1860's, but to no avail. Nevertheless, the SUR&C was now one of the largest canal companies in the country, with a total mileage of around two hundred miles linking Merseyside, Mid-Wales and the Midlands.

Although many canal companies were understandably reluctant to sell out to the railway companies, the impoverished Leominster canal was probably only too relieved when the Shrewsbury & Hereford railway offered to buy the canal in 1845. A sale was agreed in the following year, with the luckless shareholders in the canal company only receiving £16 for every £100 share. In the preamble to the Act authorising the sale, it was stated that the canal was 'of little Use for the purposes for which... (it) ... is intended'. Even then, things did not go well for the company. The S&H did not use the route of the canal after all and only agreed to honour their commitment to buy in 1858. Traffic on the canal had virtually ceased south of Wooferton as the line was crossed several times by the railway. The declining coal traffic from Blount's collieries to Wooferton itself would not pay for the upkeep of the remaining section of canal, which was formally closed in June 1858 and drained in the following year. The S&H sold this part of the canal in 1860 to the Tenbury Railway, who built their line over parts of the canal bed.

Much of the Shropshire Canal met a similar fate. Despite remaining reasonably busy it had become increasingly expensive to maintain the inclined planes and cope with the problems of poor water supply and of subsidence caused by the very mining operations that had led to its prosperity. As lessees, the SUR&C were reluctant to spend the money needed to restore the canal, estimated at around £30,000. Towards the end of 1856 the Shropshire Canal's committee were officially informed that the L&NWR were interested in buying the canal outright, in order to build a railway to Coalport. The sale was sanctioned by an Act in the following year, by which time it was reported that on the Donnington Wood incline 'The Drum-Barrel & Winding out Shaft are now so near to the Rails that the Carriage Head touches as passing under'. Apart from the section south of Tweedale Basin, near to the foot of the Windmill Farm incline, to Coalport, the rest of the Shropshire Canal (including the surviving section of the Coalbrookdale branch) officially closed in June 1858. The railway from the SUR&C line at Hadley to Coalport opened in 1861.

The remaining portion of the Shropshire Canal survived for a remarkably long time, mainly linking collieries with the ironworks at Blists Hill. It closed in stages until there was just one short length left running to the top of the Hay incline, which was abandoned by the mid-1890's but only officially closed in 1907. Even then, this short section carried nearly 30,000 tons a year until the ironworks were blown out in 1912. Although derelict after that date, it was not officially closed until 1944.

In the north of the coalfield, the Donnington Wood Canal had not been absorbed into the SUR&C and remained privately run. A short branch had been built to serve the Lodge Furnaces, probably opening in the 1840's, but the development by the Lilleshall Company of its own standard gauge railway network from the mid-1850's onwards made the canal redundant. The Lilleshall branch was abandoned in 1873 and the section east of Muxton Bridge became disused. Part of the former canal bed was used as one of the driveways to Lilleshall Hall and one of the bridges over the canal on this section was kept. After 1882, only the westernmost mile or so of the canal, leased by the Lilleshall Company, was still in use and remained so until the early years of this century.

To enable boats on this section and the short portion of the former Wombridge Canal to reach the canals still open, the rest of the Shrewsbury Canal and the Newport branch, the Trench incline had to be kept in working condition, an increasingly expensive drain on the SUR&C's resources. By the late 1860's they had decided to transfer as much of this traffic as possible to Lubstree Wharf on the Humber Arm, which had its own branch line on the Lilleshall private railway system. The company leased the wharf in 1870, paying ½d per ton to the Duke of Sutherland. Wappenshall wharf, with no rail link, was hard hit by the transfer of most of its trade to the railways after the line between Shrewsbury and Wolverhampton was opened in 1849, and by the transfer of traffic to Lubstree. The Shrewsbury Canal and the Newport branch had virtually become one since the creation of the SUR&C. Despite the heavy loss in traffic revenues, it continued to provide a useful transport link for non urgent bulky cargoes, such as coal and iron ore, and for some sundries.

The canals of the original Ellesmere Canal system in the county suffered little at first from the railway competition and actually complemented them. This was especially true of the canal link to mid-Wales and a rail/canal interchange was established at Rednal, on the Shrewsbury & Chester Railway (opened in 1848), with sidings leading down to a small arm of the Llanymynech branch. Goods to and from the mid-Wales towns and the borderland quarries were transferred between canal and rail, and for a short time, so were passengers.

Passenger traffic by canal in Shropshire seems to have been very rare. However, in 1852 the SUR&C started a service of 'Swift Passenger Boats'

An experiment by the SUR&C to introduce passenger traffic on the canals was short-lived.
(Eddowes, 8th June 1853)

connecting with trains stopping at nearby Rednal station. These 'fly' boats were hauled by several changes of horses, lighter than the usual heavy barge horses, and stopped at Maesbury (for Oswestry), Llanymynech and Welshpool en route for Newtown. The morning boat from Newtown left at 7am and arrived at Rednal just after midday.

As allies of the L&NWR, then in a bitter dispute with the Shrewsbury & Chester Railway, and no doubt proud of their canals, the company couldn't resist a dig at their rivals. A footnote to their adverts informed passengers that 'The precise times of Arrival and Departure are not guaranteed, as they must depend to some extent, on the arrival of the Railway Trains at Rednal station'. However, the service barely lasted two years, and was as unsuccessful as a similar link further north between the railway and Llangollen. The exchange sidings were lifted by the 1880's and the Bone Mill established on the site in 1858 was served by the canal.

After the initial shock of railway competition in the late 1840's, and the expansion of the railway network in the early 1860's, traffic on the county's remaining canals dwindled fairly slowly but inevitably towards the end of the nineteenth century. It was the widespread use of the motor lorry, particularly after large numbers of cheap war surplus lorries became available after the Great War, that hastened the end of the canals.

Lyneal, on a lonely stretch of the Shropshire Union in north Shropshire, in the 1960's.

In May 1917 a breach on the Weston branch of the Ellesmere Canal at Dandyfield led to its abandonment east of Hordley wharf because the L&NWR refused to finance any repair. The last tub-boat to use the Trench incline on the Shrewsbury Canal did so in August 1921 and in the following year the basin at Shrewsbury was closed, along with Lubstree Wharf on the Humber Arm.

Railways had also been hard hit by the major advances in road transport and the effects of the war, and in 1921 it was decided to merge most of them into four large regional companies, the 'Big Four'. As part of this process the SUR&C, as a dependant of the L&NWR, was merged with the parent company in 1922 and on the first day of 1923 became part of the new London, Midland and Scottish Railway. The LMS were as unsympathetic to their loss-making canal section as the L&NWR had been and did little to encourage traffic.

Although nearly 9,000 tons had been carried on the canal to Newtown in the early 1920's, by the late 1930's there were only a handful of narrowboats using the old Ellesmere sections. A major breach near to the Perry aqueduct on the Llanymynech line in February 1936 left only one boat, unloading coal at Welshpool, stranded. The LMS refused to meet their obligations to mend the breach, paid off the boat owner, and effectively abandoned the entire canal to the west of Frankton. By the late 1930's, traffic on the Newport branch and the Shrewsbury Canal had dwindled to almost nothing. The last narrowboat working into Shrewsbury itself carried tar from Oldbury to the gas works, skippered by 'Harry the Tar' until 1936. After this only a coal boat, once every six weeks or so, ventured as far westwards as Long Lane wharf and the only other craft between there and Norbury was a maintenance dredge.

The one canal in the county to stay relatively busy was the former B&LJ main line. There had even been suggestions in 1890 that this could be improved to take much larger craft, though the plans had come to nothing. It was, however, the one section left out of the wide-ranging LMS proposals officially to abandon most of the county's canals, which were ratified by a war-time Act in 1944. The line from Llantisilio through to Hurleston junction was quickly reprieved, but not for navigation. It was a vital and controllable water supply for the North-West and its miraculous preservation has proved to be a godsend to generations of holidaymakers.

As early as 1909 a Royal Commission had recommended that the canals be nationalised and radically improved. When nationalisation did eventually come, in 1948, the canals were controlled firstly by the Docks & Inland Waterways Executive of the British Transport Commission who struggled to bring order to the chaotic situation they had inherited. They were replaced in turn in 1953 by a Board of Management, and finally at the start of 1963 by the British Waterways Board. By that time the last regular traffic on the former B&LJ line had come to an end (in 1958), leaving only a handful of occasional working boats.

Since the late 1950's there has been an ever-growing revival of interest in canals and canal cruising, initially confined to enthusiasts battling through barely passable waterways. Now, increasing numbers of pleasure craft have brought new life to the canals. The canal to Llangollen is one of the most popular stretches of canal in the country. In 1974 a former clay pit off the Prees Branch near Whixall, once used to provide puddling material for the SUR&C, was converted into a boat marina and the first mile of the branch (abandoned in 1944) was re-opened.

Although plans in the 1960's to restore the canal between Norbury and Shrewsbury came too late, the story of the canal link from Frankton to Newtown, abandoned since 1936, is quite remarkable. Ambitious plans, astute fund-raising, and sheer hard (and mostly unpaid) work have already achieved remarkable results with several long sections back in water. The re-opening of Frankton Locks in 1987 was a major achievement, following hard on the heels of the restoration of those at Carreghofa. Although it will, inevitably, take time, eventually pleasure boats will be able to sample the delights of this part of the borderlands from the unique vantage point of a slow boat.

A hopeful sign - this new milepost at Frankton's upper junction
points the way to a time when it will be possible once again to
navigate all the way to Newtown.

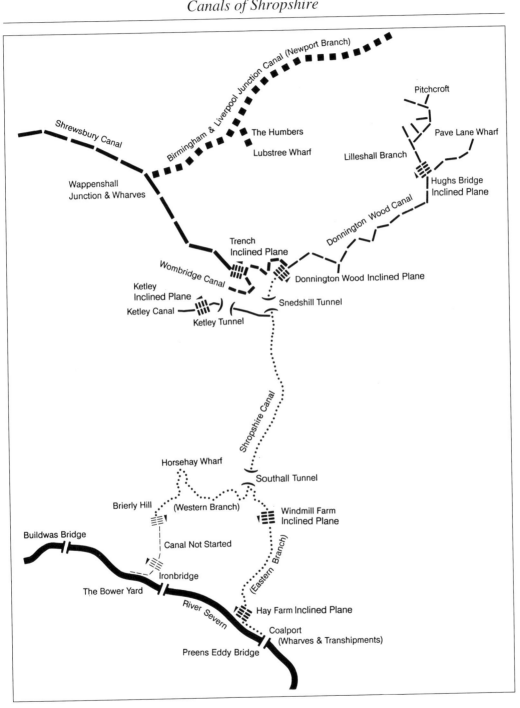

Canals in East Shropshire

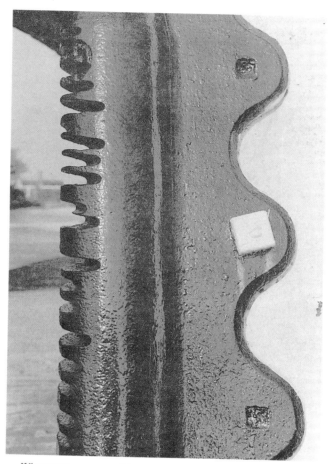

Where masonry was subject to constant wear from the tow ropes
of thousands of horse-drawn barges, it was reinforced by iron
strips which still carry the rope scars.

Canals At Work

In many ways the working life on Shropshire canals changed very little. Canal craft remained mainly horse-drawn, even though William Reynolds had been planning to power a boat on the Shropshire Canal with a steam engine shortly before his death in 1803. The Ellesmere & Chester did operate a steam tug to tow narrowboats on the B&U line in the 1840's but this was not a success. In the confines of a narrowboat, the sheer bulk of a steam engine and the space for the coal to fuel it meant the loss of too much valuable cargo space. They were also expensive to buy, operate and maintain. Only in the 1930's did diesel-engined narrowboats become common on the former B&LJ section, with a motor boat usually paired with a second, power-less narrowboat called a 'butty'. Even then the maintenance boats working from Ellesmere depot after the Second World War were still horse-drawn, and the last horse-drawn commercial narrowboats on the former B&LJ main lines were only withdrawn in 1953 - just a few years before the end of commercial trading itself.

In the early years of the canals the boats on them were owned by private carriers or industrial concerns, rather than by the canal companies themselves. Indeed, most Acts stipulated this, but did not stop those directly concerned with the canals profiting from trading on them. For example, the Shropshire Canal sold boats used in its construction to William Reynolds and John Wilkinson, and the Shrewsbury Canal sold off some of their boats used to Henry Williams. The Coalbrookdale, Lilleshall and Ketley companies all had their own fleets of tub-boats, and, after the opening of the Newport branch, they also operated narrowboats which went all over the national canal system.

In 1845 an Act allowed canal companies to act as traders as well and after their merger with B&LJ, the Ellesmere & Chester started to use their own narrowboats on the Midlands-Mersey route. The SUR&C took over and enlarged the fleet, eventually operating nearly 600 craft. The 'Shroppies' were a common sight on the national canal network until the fleet was disbanded in 1921 and sold off.

Canals carried virtually anything and everything in the first half of the nineteenth century, from foodstuffs and luxury goods to industrial raw materials. The surviving records of a wharf such as Wappenshall show the huge variety of cargoes being brought into the county - fruit, furniture, glass, soap, wine, coffee, building materials and gunpowder, just to name a few.

A lot of coal was inevitably lost during the loading and unloading of narrowboats, and these children at Whitchurch are taking advantage of the wharf owner's publicity stunt.

Ellesmere wharf in the 1920's. Already the dairy was being served by road transport and the canal basin was empty of traffic.

The principal cargoes on the early canals were coal and limestone, and coal continued to be an important cargo up until the end of commercial traffic. Coal fuelled the Industrial Revolution and in some ways limestone helped to feed it. As well as having an important role in the iron making processes, limestone was used mainly for agricultural manure, being burnt to make lime in canalside limekilns. The Llanymynech branch had mainly been built to tap the extensive limestone workings around Llanymynech, with all the major quarries linked to the canalside wharves by tramways.

Other minerals from the Welsh borders carried by the canal included slate from Oernant near Llangollen, and from the quarries in the Ceiriog valley west of Chirk which were linked to the canal by the Glyn Valley Tramway. Speed was not essential for the transport of these bulky materials, providing stock piles were kept to a reasonable level.

Apart from the industrial and mineral goods, Shropshire's canals also had considerable agricultural traffic. A thriving export trade in cheese grew up, especially in North Shropshire, with Ellesmere, Market Drayton and Whitchurch being particularly busy wharves. Milk also became an important export. Cadbury's established a factory at Knighton, on the banks of the B&LJ just outside the county, and their own fleet of narrowboats collected milk from many of the local farms on the canal until it was disbanded in 1923. A dairy plant was also set up at Ellesmere wharf towards the end of the First World War, but by the 1920's it was served mainly by lorry. Ellesmere was a major centre for malting in the mid-nineteenth century and as well as supplying its local brewing industry also supplied malt to much of Lancashire.

Malt, like cheese and milk, is a very perishable commodity and all three cargoes were carried in specially adapted narrowboats, lighter built than the standard craft. They were given special right of way at bridges and locks and often worked all round the clock with two crews. They were also given fresh teams of horses at frequent intervals along the route.

The Trench incline worked until 1921, after most of the tub-boat system had closed, to allow grain to be delivered to the flour mills at Donnington Wood by boat. On the Llanymynech branch, a malt kiln had been built by the side of the canal near to Maesbury. By the mid-nineteenth century this was a flour mill operated by the family firm of A. & A. Peate, served by a short arm off the canal. As well as using locally produced grain, by the late nineteenth century cheap North American grain had become available and was imported via Liverpool through the canal system. After the SUR&C fleet was disbanded, Peate's bought and operated 11 of the surplus narrowboats and continued to do so, despite the deteriorating condition of the canal, up until 1932 when lorries took over.

The crews of the two fundamentally different types of craft on the canals led very different ways of life. The boatmen of the tub-boat system would always work ordinary day time hours and, go home at night, when the canals were closed. The crews of the long distance narrowboats, usually just one or two men and a boy, initially had homes on shore as well, and would work in a similar way to the long-distance waggoners of the period, spending time away from their families.

It was only in the second half of the nineteenth century, when the effect of railway competition was beginning to be felt by canal companies and canal employees, that boatmen began to have their families living on board the narrowboats in extremely cramped conditions. Using family as crew members was obviously a cheaper option to a self-employed barge owner/captain (called 'Number Ones') or to a larger carrying company cutting its wage bills, and families continued to live in these cramped conditions up until the 1960's. About half of the SUR&C's fleet continued to have all-male crews, however, and in 1902 they also had two all-female crewed boats.

The travelling canal families formed a close knit community, always on the move. Looking back, their life may appear to be romantic and peaceful, but it certainly was not. Hard work and poverty went hand in hand, and in many ways those on shore treated the canal families like all too many treat gipsies today.

A family boat, with the wife opening the gate in the background, passes through Newport lock in the early years of this century whilst the horse takes a well-earned rest and feed.

Lack of education was another problem, and the typical late Victorian do-gooders saw education and religion as one and the same thing and set up a variety of societies and missions to help. In 1903, for example, the SUR&C employed a 'Lady inspector who would be able to visit the Cabins and exert a beneficial influence, especially in seeing that the children attend school'.

For obvious reasons, most canal companies banned or discouraged night time working on their canals. Sunday working was also frowned on from time to time as the companies tried to find a difficult balance between making their canals pay and satisfying the powerful religious lobby of the day. At night, and on Sundays, narrowboats were generally tied up at the canalside, their horses suitably stabled or grazing in an adjacent field, and, more often than not, their crew sampling the often dubious delights of the local hostelry and enjoying a chance to pass the time with their fellow boatmen. A place like the Canal Tavern at Welsh Frankton must have been a reasonably pleasant haven to relax in after a hard day's work on the cut.

As well as the boat crews, canals also needed a wide variety of other employees including clerks, accountants, wharfingers, lock-keepers, toll-collectors, boat-builders and repairers, carpenters and blacksmiths. In 1799 the Shropshire Canal dispensed with the services of John Vaughan, a mole-catcher! One of the most important jobs was that of the lengthsmen. These each had their own stretch of canal to patrol to make sure that everything was in working order and that there were no breaches, or potential breaches, in the canal. They would also make sure that the hedgerows by the canal were kept in check, keep the grass under control, and generally keep the towpaths tidy. Like the lock-keepers, they usually lived in canalside cottages.

CONVEYANCE
By Water.

From Thomas Harwood's Warehouse, Mardol-quay, Barges start regularly three times every week, for Bridgenorth, Bewdley, Stourport, Kidderminster, Worcester, Upton, Tewkesbury, Gloucester, Chepstow, Bristol, and all intermediate places

From Henry Newton's, Mardol-quay, by the Grand Junction Canal, to all parts on that line; by the Ellesmere Canal, from Edstaston Wharf, to all parts on that line; by the Severn, to Bridgenorth,

Merchants wishing to send their goods by water from Shrewsbury in 1822 could use the Severn, the Shrewsbury Canal, or send them overland to Edstaston Wharf on the Prees Branch of the Ellesmere & Chester.
(Pigot's "Shropshire Directory" 1822-3)

If there was a breach, or if a stretch of canal needed to be mended, a section could be isolated and drained by the use of stop planks. These were usually stored in racks by bridges along the canal. To save money, bridges were usually built with as little masonry as possible, often being little more than brick shells filled with rubble. They had very short approaches and were steeply hump-backed. There was usually only enough room for one narrowboat to pass beneath the bridge hole. A pair of vertical iron grooves on either side of the canal took the ends of the stop planks, and once fitted, the water could be drained away where needed - usually through one of the many overflow sluices.

Keeping the locks in good repair was another vital maintenance task and required a considerable degree of skill from the carpenters in particular, as the gates were usually made of wood. Telford had recommended the use of iron lock gates on the Ellesmere Canal and in 1822 the Committee were told that the first of these had been installed at Frankton, followed by others at New Marton and Aston, and that 'the general adoption of which (is) strongly recommended'. Whatever their advantages all were later replaced by conventional timber gates.

The canal companies had a duty, and of course a need, to keep their canals in good order, though often the lack of sufficient income meant that this was difficult. Apart from the occasional breach in the canal bank, the most common problem was the freezing up of the slow moving water in the canal in severe winters. To combat this, each company had one, and usually several ice-breakers. These specially made boats had keels (unlike the usually flat-bottomed narrowboats and tub-boats) and a large 'goal-post' frame running their length. Men would cling to this and rock the boat from side to side as a team of horses pulled it as fast as possible through the ice. It was a spectacular sight. However, not all companies were too concerned to keep the canals ice-free, especially before the competition of the railways made itself felt. For example, in August 1821 the Shrewsbury Canal decided not to break the ice on the canal in the following winter at all.

Canals made the most of their money by charging a fixed amount for each ton of cargo carried by each boat between fixed quarter mile posts along the canal, and a system of painted figures of copper strips fixed to the hulls evolved. These showed the normal displacement of the boat unloaded and the different waterline levels at different cargo weights, which would then be 'tallied' by the toll-collectors along the route. Usually on the narrowboats several 'tally strips' were fixed to the hull to allow for unevenly loaded vessels and an average reading taken.

After the creation of the SUR&C most of the county's canals were administered from Ellesmere. In 1805 the Ellesmere Canal company decided 'to erect a Canal Office at Ellesmere being the most central point on the Navigation'. Now called Beech House, this stands guarding the junction of the Ellesmere branch and is a fine late Georgian building with a peculiar three-quarter round bow at its northern corner. On the ground floor, this contained a Committee Room and elsewhere in the building were an accounts office, a plans store, and 'apartments connected therewith for the resident Accountant, Agent and the resident Engineer'. This may well have been designed by Telford.

Nearby a maintenance depot was established, which is still used by the British Waterways Board, although with only a fraction of the staff that once would have worked here. As well as having its own dry dock for boat repair, and for boat building, this depot built and repaired lock gates and produced in its carpenters' shops and smithy all the paraphernalia needed by a large, widespread concern such as the SUR&C.

The former Shropshire Union maintenance depot at Ellesmere is still used
by the British Waterways Board, though not as busy as it once was.

The headquarters of the other companies appear to have been much more modest
affairs, often little more than maintenance depots by the canalside. The Donnington
Wood had a boatyard by the side of a basin near to Lilleshall Abbey, and a second by
another basin at Whixall. The Shrewsbury Canal's headquarters were at the Shrewsbury
Basin, whilst the Shropshire Canal had their main headquarters, warehouse and
manager's house at Snedshill. The impoverished Leominster Canal built a fairly grand
building, the Wharf House, at Marlbrook Wharf, but their boat repairs were probably
carried out at Tenbury.

A restored working narrowboat leaves Tyrley top lock heading north towards Market Drayton.

Canals Today

The best way to see the navigable canals of Shropshire is from a narrowboat or pleasure cruiser, and the best way to see its rivers is by canoe or rowing boat. However, there is also plenty to see from the towpath and the county's rivers and canals run through beautiful and varied scenery. Even the once bleak industrial landscapes of East Shropshire have become attractive in an odd sort of way as nature claims its own.

There are few relics of the Severn's river traffic above Shrewsbury, and even in the county town only fragmentary traces of the old wharves survive. However, the towpath arches of the Welsh and English bridges are still there, as is the old barge gutter across Frankwell meadows. Downstream, at low water, traces of the fish weir at Preston Boats can still be seen.

It is often difficult to believe that the horse towpath ever existed. Its most tangible remains are the bridges carrying the path over small brooks at Leighton, Eardington and Highley. It is still possible to follow stretches of the river on a public footpath that dates back to medieval times, but how other portions of this ancient right of way have been extinguished is a mystery. Incidentally, the Severn is one of the very few rivers in England and Wales that is a free navigation and so can still be used by anyone at any time.

Remains of the River Tern's pound-lock at Attingham exist, close to the confluence with the Severn. Predictably the Ironbridge Gorge has the best preserved features of the navigation. The Coalbrookdale Company's mock-Gothic warehouse at Loadcroft Wharf, built in the 1840's, is now appropriately a Museum of the River run by the Ironbridge Gorge Museum Trust. In the Gorge, remains of some of the warehouses, wharves and factories served by the river can still be seen. Further downstream there are few traces, but the scenery is superb.

Whether they are waterways bustling with pleasure cruisers or dry and derelict reminders of a forgotten past, canals can be fascinating to walk along. The county's two surviving canal routes are amongst the most popular for canal cruisers and there is also plenty to keep the towpath stroller and the lockside loafer (or 'gongoozler') interested.

The former B&LJ line is now universally known as the Shropshire Union, or 'Shroppie', and heading northwards crosses into Shropshire near Knighton. After the green gloom of the Woodseaves Cutting it emerges at Tyrley Wharf. For several hundred yards the towpath marks the county boundary and the canal itself is actually in Staffordshire. At Tyrley the canalside buildings are restored and with crews preparing for the descent down, or recovering from the climb up the five Tyrley locks, it is, in summer, a fine spot for watching canal life go by.

Another rocky cutting leads to Market Drayton and its busy wharf, past which is the short cutting through Betton Wood, reputed to be haunted. Beyond the wood is the beautifully kept flight of five locks at Adderley complete with flower beds. The canal then crosses into Cheshire and descends the fifteen lock flight down past Audlem.

Morris's Bridge, on the former Ellesmere Canal near Whixall, is one of the new hydraulic steel lift bridges that at least echo the style of the wooden ones they are gradually replacing.

The waterway between Hurleston and Llantisilio is now simply called the Llangollen Canal and crosses the county border at Grindley Brook, where three ordinary locks and one staircase lock (similar to that at Frankton) lift boats 40 feet in a few hundred yards. The lock-keeper's house with its bow window was probably designed by Telford, who considered himself an architect as well as an engineer. After the junction for the long abandoned Whitchurch branch, the canal crosses atmospheric Whixall Moss.

The bleakness of the scenery is enlivened by the wooden Dutch-style lift bridges, so common on the continent but quite rare in Britain, introduced by the Ellesmere Canal to save money. Gradually these are being replaced by modern steel equivalents with hydraulic lifting gear, and just past one of these, Morris's Bridge at Whixall, is the junction for the Prees Branch guarded by a three storey canal house.

The Prees branch had been disused long before it was officially closed in 1944 but the first mile, which has two lift bridges is navigable once again and leads to a marina. Part of the watered section beyond the marina is now a nature reserve, but the canal bed is dry past Edstaston where some of the wharf buildings have survived. There are also fragmentary remains of the roadside wharf at Quina Brook.

The main line of the canal runs in a virtual straight line from the junction to Bettisfield, crosses briefly into Wales. and then winds through Shropshire's own 'Lake District', skirting both Colemere and Blakemere before entering the short (87 yds.) Ellesmere Tunnel. Beyond is the junction with the Ellesmere branch, Beech House (the former SUR&C offices), and the British Waterways Board maintenance depot. The Ellesmere branch can be full of moored pleasure craft in the summer but the recent closure of the dairy has taken away some of its liveliness. The town wharf has been restored and one of the warehouses still advertises the Shropshire Union's services.

At Frankton, the canal joins the former Ellesmere main line, and after the widely spaced pair of locks at New Marton, heads for the Welsh hills. Chirk aqueduct is now overshadowed by its taller companion, a railway viaduct built in 1848. Halfway across is the county, and country border but anyone in a boat, or indeed on foot, should try to finish the next few miles of the route. Crossing the very symbol of canal engineering, the Pontcysyllte aqueduct over the Dee is a must for any boater and a test of courage for anyone with a healthy respect for heights. Beyond the aqueduct, the pretty feeder from Llantisilio is navigable to Llangollen.

For the most part, the towpaths of the navigable portions of the old Shropshire Union are in good condition and walking them is easy. This cannot be said of the disused canals, where sturdy boots and thick socks are needed to cope with the mud and the undergrowth. Matters are improving all the time, however, on the former Llanymynech branch of the SUR&C. This now seems to have taken on a new semi-official, but incorrect, name - the Montgomery Canal. The old warehouse and wharf crane at the top junction at Frankton have long gone, but the check house by the restored locks has been renovated. The lock-keeper's house and the old Canal Tavern are now both private houses, but the former boatbuilder's cottage is derelict and the dry dock nearby, used for boat repairs as late as the 1930's, is overgrown.

At the bottom junction work has begun on the next phase of the restoration. The Ellesmere's proposed main line turned eastwards at the lower junction, heading for

Shrewsbury and the Severn. Despite ploughing, much of the line is still visible, although most of the bridges have gone. The basin at Hordley is unrecognisable, but there are interesting canal remains, including lime-kilns and a warehouse, at Weston Wharf.

The Llanymynech branch is easy to follow. The first bridge, Lockgate Bridge, is surely the most hump-backed of hump-backed bridges and should be treated with great caution by any car driver. The old Perry Aqueduct still stands but will probably be replaced when the canal is restored. At Rednal was the short lived rail/canal interchange basin later used by a fertilizer factory. Here also is the curious partially timber-framed canalside building generally considered to be the terminus of the short lived 'Swift Passenger Boats' service to Newport. It is by a fine stone roving bridge; the towpath at this point changes sides, the bridge being designed to allow the horses to cross the canal, without having to let go of the tow.

This partially timber-framed building at Rednal is usually thought to be the passenger terminal of the short-lived fly boat service to Newtown. Beyond is a fine roving bridge, allowing horses to cross the canal when the towpath changed sides without loosing the tow.

At Queen's Head there was a sand pit and a flour mill, but the old Holyhead Road (A5) bridge was demolished many years ago and the canal culverted. The village has recently been by-passed, and it is gratifying to see that the new road bridge was built to allow narrowboats to pass beneath it once the canal has been restored, and even has timber rubbing strakes, ready at water level to cope with badly steered barges! A long straight leads past the widely spaced trio of Aston locks, currently being restored. Between the lower locks are the rotting remains of an iron sheeted wooden boat, presumably an old ice-breaker.

Despite losing its warehouse in a fire, Maesbury Marsh still has the atmosphere of a canalside village, helped no doubt by the restored crane on its wharfside and the Navigation Inn by the bridge. Maesbury Mill, served by the last fleet of working boats on the branch, is nearby and the site of the short arm that served it is still visible. Just to the east a slight widening of the canal bed marks the site of Gronwen Wharf, terminus of the Morda Tramway which ran westwards to coal pits around Sweeney Mountain. There are more substantial remains of a wharf at Crickheath, the terminus of the older Crickheath tramway, which probably opened at the same time as the canal and served limestone quarries around Porthywaen.

A whole series of shorter tramways and inclines ran down the flank of Llanymynech Hill and the exploration of this area will delight anyone with an interest in industrial archaeology. The main road through Llanymynech also marks the border between England and Wales, and shortly after crossing that border, the Llanymynech branch joined the Montgomeryshire just above the locks at Carreghofa.

The former B&LJ Newport branch has not fared as well, although its junction with the main line at Norbury is still a busy canal centre and the remains of the Norbury flight of locks are nearby. The canal crosses the Shropshire border just to the east of Newport and has been partially restored as part of a landscaping scheme in the town itself. However, it quickly becomes derelict further west and is difficult to walk. Lubstree Wharf at the end of the Humber Arm is remarkably intact and the basin in water. A bridge, wharf cottage and transhipment shed complete a scene that is just lacking narrowboats. The canal ends at Wappenshall Junction where the large warehouse, wharf and magnificent roving bridge all survive.

Long sections of the former Shrewsbury Canal to the west of the junction have been filled in, and many of the bridges demolished. Part of the old canal is used for drainage and Eyton Mill lock is again in water; nearby is a rather pretty brick lock-keeper's house. The Roden aqueduct at Rodington is no more, but its long approach embankment, incorporating a single arch brick aqueduct, survives. The famous iron aqueduct at Longden-on-Tern still stands and, fortunately, plans to move it have been abandoned. However, it is a pity that such an important monument is not yet served by a good layby on the road, a good footpath to it, and an informative display panel.

Many of the canal buildings at Berwick Wharf remain and a rough walk along the remains of the towpath alongside the marshy canal leads to the bricked up east portal of the Berwick Tunnel. The west portal, in Preston is easier to get to and in between are two of the ventilation shafts. With the flank of Haughmond Hill always in view, the approach

Ditherington Mill was built as a flax works alongside the new Shrewsbury Canal in 1796. The first iron-framed building in the world, it was later converted to a maltings, still served by the canal until this century. This photograph probably dates from the nineteen hundreds.

By 1954, work had started on filling in this section of the canal. Factory Bridge had been rebuilt in 1913, and the top of Ditherington Mill can be seen beyond it. The lads by the bridge are as curious of the photographer as their predecessors half a century earlier.

to Shrewsbury is very pleasant, although walking is only practicable after Uffington. At Ditherington, the canal passes the Maltings, now empty and awaiting a new use after two centuries. This is another industrial monument of national importance: the first iron-framed factory in the world. The basin in Shrewsbury has long been filled in, but there is still a Canal Tavern, and the former Butter Market at the canal head has recently been converted into a night club.

The southernmost section of the Shrewsbury Canal will, hopefully, be partially restored as part of a long term scheme to enhance this area of Telford New Town. The remains of the locks survive, and two in Hadley Park still retain the headgear supporting the guillotine locks. There are few traces of the Trench Incline, although Trench Pool is still in existence and used for sailing.

A combination of railway building in the nineteenth century and the creation of the new town from the mid-1960's onwards has meant that many of the traces of the former tub-boat system in the Telford area have been obliterated, which makes finding them that much more satisfying. The first canal, the Donnington Wood, has few real features of interest left, apart from the remains of both the incline and the former tunnel and shaft system at Hugh's Bridge. A section of the canal was converted into a drive to Lilleshall Abbey, now a National Sports Centre. The Lilleshall branch can be traced with care, as can the latter branch to the Old Lodge furnaces, in Granville Country Park.

Odd stretches of the northern portion of the Shropshire Canal are still visible, but there is little to see of the old Ketley Canal that joined it. At Southall, the tunnel was destroyed when the railway was built, but is remembered in the name of a terrace of houses nearby. The junction between the Western and Eastern branches has not survived. The first portion of the Western branch can be easily walked and includes the aqueduct that gives this part of the new town its name. After disappearing into a housing estate the canal reappears, occasionally in water, by Dawley Castle and can be traced as far as Doseley. The loop up towards Horsehay has gone, but there are further traces, including a well preserved bridge, all the way to Brierly Hill where the Coalbrookdale Company's incline is clearly visible.

On the Eastern branch there are few remains of note until Blists Hill Museum, where the canal has been restored all the way to the top of the Hay Incline above Coalport. Traces of the winding house buildings and the top-locks have survived and standard gauge rails have been laid on the slope to recreate the feel of this impressive relic of the canal age. The bottom section at Coalport runs past the Coalport China Works, now one of the IGMT's museums, as is Reynold's Tar Tunnel nearby.

Along the southern boundary of the county, tracing the remains of the ill-fated Leominster Canal is surprisingly rewarding and has the benefit of very pleasant scenery. Most of the line from Wooferton to Mamble can be traced, although the locks have been filled in. The central arch of the Teme Aqueduct was blown up as an Army exercise in the Second World War, but the Rea Aqueduct does survive in poor condition. The fine Wharf House near Marlbrook is a reminder of the unfulfilled ambitions of the canal mania. There are slight traces of the canal to the east, near the site of the west portal of the Southnet Tunnel, and at Dumbleton Farm. Better stretches of the canal survive in Herefordshire, and the northern portal of the Putnal Fields tunnel is in good condition - perhaps best seen from the trains on the Shrewsbury-Hereford line.

Postscript

For the time being, the prospect for the county's canals seems good. More and more people are taking to the rivers and canals in all sorts of craft, and restoration of the 'Montgomery Canal' continues. Legislation now protects the important monuments such as Longden and Chirk aqueducts, and Wappenshall Wharf. However, no-one has ever accurately predicted the future of canals. How many of the thousands flocking to invest in the Ellesmere Canal realised that it would never be finished? Who would have thought that the prosperous Shropshire Canal would last barely half a century? Conversely, who, even in the 1940's, would have believed the interest in canals today, or that people would willingly give up their free time to restore the canals that were then being abandoned? Given the growing awareness of 'green' issues, can we today rule out the possibility of bulky goods once again being carried on inland navigations, and the creation of an improved network of environmentally friendly canals in an integrated national transport system? For the present, our inland waterways, used or disused, provide an important leisure amenity at a time when leisure time is, for whatever reason, on the increase. Long may they continue to do so.

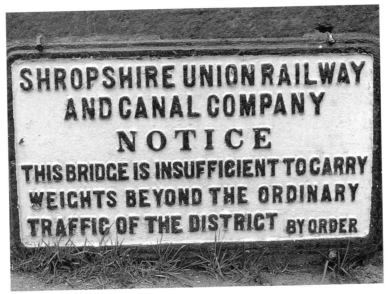

Cast iron canal signs have proven remarkably resilient, the main threat to them being from thieves who steal them to sell to collectors - who should know better.

Suggested Further Reading

Local Books

Denton, J. Horsley,	'A Towpath Guide to the Montgomeryshire Canal and the Llanymynech Branch of the Ellesmere Canal'
Hadfield, C.,	'The Canals of the West Midlands'
Pearson's	'Canal Companion: Llangollen and Shropshire Union'
Pellow, T. & Bowen, P.,	'Canal to Llangollen'
Trinder, B.S.,	'The Industrial Revolution in Shropshire'
Webb, M.,	'Shroppie Boats'
Wilson, E.,	'The Ellesmere and Llangollen Canals'

General Books

Gladwin, D.D.,	'The Waterways of Britain: A Social Panorama'
Hadfield, C.,	'British Canals'
Hadfield, C.,	'The Canal Age'
McKnight, H.,	'The Shell Book of Inland Waterways'
Ransom, P.1G.,	'The Archaeology of Canals'
Rolt, LT.C.,	'Navigable Waterways'
Russel, R.,	'Lost Canals and Waterways of Britain'
Squires, R.W.,	'The New Navvies: A History of the Modern Waterways'

More books on transport published by Shropshire Books

'Shropshire Railways Pictorial' compiled by the Shropshire Railways Society
Paperback £5.50

'Railways of Shopshire' Richard K Morriss.
Paperback. £5.99

'Historic Bridges of Shropshire' Anthony Blackwall. Hardback. £4.25

For a complete list of Shropshire Books titles, please write to:
Shropshire Books, Column House, 7 London Road, Shrewsbury SY2 6NW.